The PATH *to* WISDOM

GUIDANCE *for* HUMANITY

Saeida Rouass

THE ISLAMIC FOUNDATION

Published by

The Islamic Foundation
Markfield Conference Centre
Ratby Lane, Markfield
Leicestershire, LE67 9SY, United Kingdom
Tel: 01530 244944/5, Fax: 01530 244946
E-mail: info@islamic-foundation.org.uk
publications@islamic-foundation.com
Website: www.islamic-foundation.org.uk

Quran House, P.O. Box 30611, Nairobi, Kenya

P.M.B. 3193, Kano, Nigeria

British Library Cataloguing-in-Publication Data

Rouass, Saeida
The path to wisdom: guidance for humanity
1. Muslims – Religious life 2. Muslims – Conduct of life
I. Title II. Islamic Foundation (Great Britain)
297.5'7

ISBN 0 86037 575 7

We thank the following persons for their contribution in providing us with the photographs:
Adam Williamson, Batool Al-Toma, Nasir Cadir, Sakir Cadir and Vaseem Mohammed

Cover/Book design & typeset: Nasir Cadir
Printed & bound in England: Antony Rowe Ltd

Dedication

For my mother and father,

For always challenging me to think for myself.

Transliteration Table

Arabic Consonants:

Initial, unexpressed medial and final:

ء	ʾ	د	d	ض	ḍ	ك	k
ب	b	ذ	dh	ط	ṭ	ل	l
ت	t	ر	r	ظ	ẓ	م	m
ث	th	ز	z	ع	ʿ	ن	n
ج	j	س	s	غ	gh	هـ	h
ح	ḥ	ش	sh	ف	f	و	w
خ	kh	ص	ṣ	ق	q	ي	y

Vowels, diphthongs, etc.

Short:	ـَ	a	ـِ	i	ـُ	u
Long:	ـَا	ā	ـُو	ū	ـِي	ī
Diphthongs:			ـِوْ	aw		
			ـَىْ	ay		

بسم الله الرحمن الرحيم

Contents

Acknowledgements

The idea for this book jumped out at me at a crossroads in my life. I found myself in a place that pushed me to question what I thought I knew. I realised that Islam was something outside of me, and that though I consciously lived a Muslim lifestyle, I had never really allowed its teachings into the very core of me.

I would like to thank Allah, al-Fattāḥ (SWT), for taking me to that crossroads. I know that in His Wisdom Allah took me to a precipice and compelled me to look over the edge. And then in His Mercy He opened up the horizon that existed inside me, that exists inside all of us.

This book became the backbone of a personal journey. As I compiled it I discovered an internal and external world that flooded me with light and hope. As I walked along the path of self-reflection, through the teachings of Islam, I could feel the presence of Allah guiding me, creating obstacles and then removing them effortlessly, for my benefit alone. I am humbled that Allah, al-Ḥalīm, made this journey possible and did not forsake me. I cannot thank Him enough for all that working on this book has done for my soul.

In His Generosity, Allah (SWT) has surrounded me by wonderful people that have offered help, support and encouragement at different stages in the preperation of the manuscript.

I am fortunate to have a family that nurtures my aspirations. Laila's refusal to accept anything but my best efforts, Mohammed and Kay's instant pride and Aunty Kim's utter belief in me have all been pivotal and deeply touching.

My heart-felt thanks go to Fatima Khan and Sultana Begum for being there from the very beginning with observations, comments and positive criticisms. Your genuine love for the manuscript and its message inspired me through the various stages. If no one else got it, I knew that you two did.

I am indebted to Arif Zubair for finding time in his busy schedule to do the first proofread and for helping with the technical aspects of writing. Thank you for never tiring of having your brain picked.

The encouragement I have had from friends has touched me and while I cannot mention them all, I must at least mention Zohra, Bibi and Shazia.

I would like to thank the Library staff at the Islamic Cultural Centre in London for always taking the time to answer my questions and putting at my disposal all that they could. In particular thanks to Doctor Adel M Abbas for his words of wisdom and giving me access to the Library when it was closed to the public. The patient help in locating relevant manuscripts by staff at the British Library is also much appreciated.

I would also like to thank all the publishing staff at the Islamic Foundation. In particular I am indebted to Anwar Cara for his valuable advice and comments and immensely grateful to Professor Kidwai for his guidance and recommendations.

Finally, the numerous thinkers quoted in this book, and those that have preserved their work, have enriched me forever.

Through their legacies each has dared me to take on the challenge of conscious existence and walk my path to wisdom. I pray that Allah rewards them all for their efforts.

Introduction

"Praise be to God, alone in His Majesty and His Might, and unique in His Sublimity and His Everlastingness, who clips the wings of intellects well short of the glow of His Glory, and who makes the way of knowing Him through the inability to know Him; who makes the tongues of the eloquent fall short of praising the beauty of His presence unless they use the means by which He praises Himself, and use His names and attributes which He has enumerated. And may blessings be upon Muḥammad, the best of His creatures, and on his Companions and his family."[1]

In the Glorious Qur'ān Allah, the Most High, says:

"It is He who creates you out of dust, and then out of a drop of sperm, and then out of a germ-cell; and then He brings you forth as children; and then (He ordains) that you reach maturity, and then that you grow old – though some of you (He causes to) die earlier – and (all this He ordains) so that you might reach a term set by Him and that you might (learn to) use your reason."[2]

The Holy Qur'ān and the illuminating *Aḥādīth* of Muḥammad, the Messenger of God (peace be upon him), contain numerous references to the need for reflection and thought. Some indicate their vital importance to a meaningful existence while others highlight the use of thought to see the signs *of*, and messages *from* God in the universe and in our lives.

Indeed, the concepts of intellect and reflection are at the very root of what it means to be a human being and without the active and conscious use of the mind, man and woman are doomed to live only a limited existence.

Through reflection on the guidance sent down from our Most Merciful Lord, what we *do* and what we *are*, we can elevate our existence to a higher realm characterised by righteousness and noble morality. When man and woman act only on whim and impulse their existence is lowered to a realm characterised by individualism and ill-conceived choices.

Consequently, Islamic literature from the past and present is rich with knowledge and wisdom; aroused by the understanding that without reflecting on our religious text and personal journeys through life we can gain no lessons to guide us and future generations to a more inspired existence.

Each successive generation produces its own reality, needs and circumstances and the people of that time respond accordingly. This is no more apparent than in Islamic history, from which scholars, leaders, guides and writers have emerged to correct our mistakes and redirect us to the path of God.

Such people perceived the world around them, the diseases of their time and took the action necessary to ebb the flow of our own self-destruction. And grateful we are for that.

The men and women quoted in this book are examples of some of those people; who understood that in order to save themselves they must learn, and were generous enough to pass on their reflections to a needy audience.

The lessons they preach and the wisdom they arrived at is timeless. It spoke to the listeners in their mosques, schools, markets, royal courts and battlefields with the same resounding truth that it speaks to us today in our homes, universities, offices and global communication networks.

In the simple but penetrating words of al-Junayd:

"These are our works, these works our souls display. Behold our works when we have passed away."[3]

The wisdom of what they preach, despite being a product of the circumstances within which they found themselves, transcends the limits of space and time and reaches up to universal truth and human nature.

While some were driven by the internal world of the self and a need to understand their place in the universe, others felt compelled to respond to the external world and the social, political and spiritual crises of their time.

What makes each of them remarkable is not the extent of their knowledge but rather what they chose to do with it and their insatiable thirst for knowing. Each was aware that the depths of their understanding were merely drops in the ocean of Allah's unfolding revelation of us to ourselves.

Those quoted were involved in different aspects of Islamic learning and life, and the book includes a range of thinkers. This aims to create a balance of thought so that no one science or perspective dominates. Instead, it seeks to establish that despite the various and sometimes conflicting views of the writers, essentially they all agreed on certain undeniable principles.

The format of this book is designed to move in a natural progression, from the starting point of meaningful existence: Reflection, to the end of that existence: Death. It seeks to encompass the multi-faceted nature of life and consequently each chapter deals with a certain aspect of our being.

Part One reflects on the self and the relationship we have with our conscience.

Part Two deals with the relationship we have with our Creator and the issues that affect its condition.

Part Three reflects on our relationship with mankind and on the Islamic principles that should influence how we conduct ourselves with others.

Finally, Part Four looks at our place in the world around us, and how we respond to all that it brings.

The chapters are in no way exhaustive of human experience or of the perceptions of those quoted.

Each chapter is headed by a *Ḥadīth* of the Prophet Muḥammad (peace be upon him) as a mark of respect for the nobility of his perfect example.

The best example for mankind and the one that started the tradition, in Islam, of pondering the guidance of Allah, the Most High, in all its forms, it seems only fitting that the words of those that followed in his reflective footsteps should proceed from his own.

The book also includes short profiles of those quoted with further reading, so that the reader may learn more about the lives of these most enlightened thinkers.

The quotes have not been placed according to the rank or nobility of the individuals referenced but according to their appropriateness in the wider context of the book and life. Therefore, I hope you, the reader, will look beneath each individual quote and find the hidden thread that links them all together.

This book started from a personal journey and a realisation that all that I knew of Islam was through an uncritical acceptance of the ideas and views circulating within my world. I desired to break my boundaries of awareness and understood the only way to do that was to search for the truth in everything, reflect on what was before me and ultimately trust that Allah would lead me to a better place. Allah, the Expander, chose to lead me here.

I soon realised that what we know or come to know is not new, but the cyclic revelation of human nature, repeating itself to each successive generation. And that the internal and external struggles of man and woman may vary in the detail but all ultimately lead to the same universal truths, behind which lies the ultimate truth of God.

I urge you, the reader, to take on the noble task of self-reflection and hope the book that you now hold will act only to deepen your awareness and understanding. I hope that you will ponder on each quote and derive your own meaning with an open mind and heart, and that the wisdom contained in these pages will become a part of who you are and follow you wherever you go.

To end…or should I say, to begin:

"All that is left to us from tradition is mere words. It is up to us to find out what they mean."[4]

Saeida Rouass

I
The Self

1

Reflection

Ibn ʿAbbās (may Allah be well pleased with him) narrated that the Messenger (peace be upon him) said:

> "O ʿAbd al-Qays! In the character there are two traits that God and His Messenger love, namely mildness and deliberation."[5]

Ḥadīth

Indeed man should reflect deeply over his creation, his physically and physiologically perfect constitution.

Reflection should prompt him to show his genuine gratitude, deep respect and real love to Allah, his Gracious Lord, who has blessed him with such constitution, perfect, upright and handsome.

Sayyid Quṭb[6]

Remember the True One and His actions of management over His Creatures. Reflect on His Mastership and Greatness.

Reflect on that when you have withdrawn from the company of your families and when other eyes have gone to sleep.

Al-Jīlānī[7]

One who thinks and reflects develops his foresight and vision.

ʿAlī ibn Abī Ṭālib[8]

By self-examination the slave attains the rank of self-domination.[9]

Abū Madyan[10]

Let man consider his origins and what has become of him.

Sayyid Quṭb[11]

You must reflect on your life and where it is likely to lead you.

Al-Jīlānī[12]

A devout personage had bowed his head on the breast of contemplation and was immersed in the ocean of the divine presence.

When he came back to himself from that state one of his companions sportily asked him, "From that flower garden where you were, what miraculous gift have you brought for us?"

He replied, "I intended to fill my lap as soon as I should reach the rose trees and bring presents for you, my companions. When I arrived there the fragrance of the roses so intoxicated me that the skirt of my robe slipped from my hands."[13]

Shaykh Saʿdī[14]

The failure to attain perception is itself perception.[15]

Abū Bakr[16]

2

Knowledge

Ibn ʿAbbās reported (may Allah be well pleased with him), the Messenger of Allah (peace be upon him) said (to a group of Companions):

"When you pass by the meadows of Paradise indulge freely in it."

They said: "O Messenger of Allah, what are the meadows of Paradise?"

He replied "The circles of Knowledge."[17]

Ḥadīth

Walk in search of knowledge and knowledgeable persons until no further walking is possible.

Keep walking until your legs no longer obey you. So, when you become unable to walk, sit down with your outward, then with your inward, then with your heart and then with your essence. When you become totally exhausted, outwardly and inwardly and have to sit, nearness of Allah and attainment to Him will come to you.

Al-Jīlānī[18]

They say to me that you are withdrawn, but they saw a man even more humiliated and withdrawn.

I saw people who belittled any humble soul who drew near to them; anyone that was exalted by pride, they received with honour.

I gave not knowledge its due.

And every time a craving of the world came to me, I used my knowledge as a staircase to attain it.

When it was said: "This is a fountain", I said, "I see", but the unfettered soul will (foolishly) endure thirst.

I strove not in the service of knowledge, nor as a servant to the needy souls I met.

I sought, instead, to be served.

And I to be made wretched by the seedling I planted, harvesting only humiliation.

If this is so, it would have been better to seek ignorance.

If only the people of knowledge had protected it, it would have protected them.

If they had magnified it in their souls, they would have been magnified.

To the contrary, they belittled it, and therefore became despicable.

They disfigured its face with their craving for the world, leaving it frowning and dejected.

Al-Jurjānī[19]

And now I see learning like heavy clouds wide spread above you, rich with promise of life giving water; their deep shadows foretelling imminent rain and your hopes high for it.
Seek then the rain which is in the clouds and wait patiently where it will fall.

And make your plea to God, who brings on the rain, who spreads wide the clouds, who removes famine, who gives freedom to the bound.[20]

Junayd[21]

If you desire to gain what is with Allah with your quest for knowledge, than you have obtained what will benefit you. If you desire to gain this world by your learning, than your hands will remain empty.

Mālik ibn Anas[22]

Whoever learns the Qur'ān has immense value.
Whoever cites *Ḥadīth* strengthens his proof.
Whoever studies *fiqh* has noble stature.
Whoever examines language refines his nature.
Whoever considers the Reckoning has sound opinion.
Whoever does not protect himself, does not benefit from his knowledge.

Al-Shāfiʿī[23]

The best knowledge is the knowledge of Allah, His names, attributes and actions.

This knowledge engenders in its possessor direct knowledge of Allah, His fear, His love, His reverence, His exaltation, His magnification, intense devotion, absolute reliance on Him, being pleased with Him and preoccupation with Him.

Ibn Rajab al-Ḥanbalī[24]

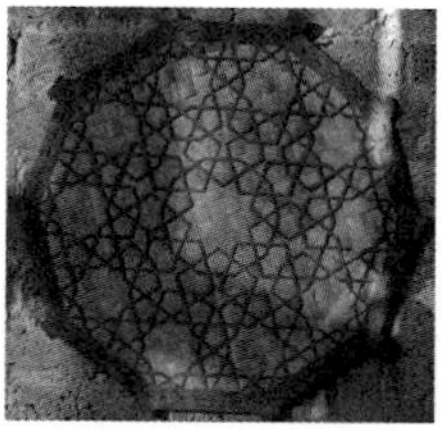

Know that the first condition of worship of God – may He be exalted and magnified – is knowledge of God and that the basis of knowledge of God is the recognition of His being One and that His unity demands the absolute negation of the possibility of describing God in answer to the questions: How? Where? and When?[25]

Junayd[26]

The ultimate knowledge of the 'knowers' lies in their inability to know. In their realising in fact, that they do not know Him and that it is utterly impossible for them to know Him. Indeed, that it is impossible for anyone except God to know God.[27]

Al-Ghazālī[28]

Whoever knows all things without knowing God – Great and Glorious – is not worthy to be called wise because he does not know the most sublime and highest of all things.

Al-Ghazālī[29]

Whoever knows God – the Most High – is wise, even if his aptitude is deficient in the other conventional modes of knowledge, or his speech is slow or faltering in expanding them.

Al-Ghazālī[30]

A learned man who doesn't restrain his passions is like a blind man holding a torch, he guides others but not himself.

Shaykh Saʿdī[31]

3
Character and Self-Awareness

Shaddād (may Allah be well pleased with him) narrated that the Messenger of Allah (peace be upon him) said:

"The intelligent man is he who contemplates his self and acts for what is after death; and he is the weak man who makes his soul follow his lust."[32]

Ḥadīth

Know that you are your own veil, which conceals your self from you. Know also, that you cannot reach God through yourself, but that you reach God through Him.[33]

Junayd[34]

Know that the man that is dominated by sloth will consider unpleasant any spiritual struggle and discipline or any purifying of the soul and refinement of character.

Because of his deficiency and remissness and the foulness of his inward nature, his soul will not permit him to undertake such a thing.

Therefore, he will claim that the traits of a man's character cannot be conceivably altered and that human nature is immutable.

Al-Ghazālī[35]

It is said that when God wants to transport a servant from the humiliation of disobedience to the honour of obedience He makes him familiar with solitude, enriches him with contentment and brings him to see the shameful deeds of his own ego.

Al-Qushayrī[36]

Know O Dear Readers that God shows evil to one for whom He wishes good.

He has no fear that has insight. When a man can know his own faults he can try to remove them. But the majority of men remain ignorant of their faults.

Al-Ghazālī[37]

If a person can see and acknowledge his own deficiencies he will come to experience perfection. But if someone admires his own perfection, he will end up with nothing but deficiency.

Al-Jīlānī[38]

Never have I dealt with anything more difficult than my own soul, which sometimes helps me and sometimes opposes me.

Al-Ghazālī[39]

Remember that it is harder to tame the self than to tame wild beasts. In fact, when wild beasts are shut inside cages ordered for them by kings, they cannot harm you.

But the self, even if it were put in a prison, could not be guaranteed to do you no harm.

Ibn Ḥazm[40]

May God have mercy on him who brings me my faults as a present.

ʿUmar ibn al-Khaṭṭāb[41]

O Allah!
You know my self better than I do, and I know my self better than they do.
O Allah!
Make me better than what they think, and do not take me to task for what they say.

Abū Bakr[42]

4
Whims and Desires

Abū Dharr (may Allah be well pleased with him) said that the Messenger of Allah (peace be upon him) said:

> "The best form of Jihād is a man who fights against himself and his desire."[43]

Ḥadīth

Whoever conquers the passion of his soul has conquered all men. No one has any power over him, since the goal of his enemies is to try to annihilate his body, yet that person lives for his spirit. Whoever dies to his passions in this life will live in his death.[44]

Al-Ghazālī[45]

Alas! People have gone to rack and ruin through their own fond hopes and daydreams.

They talk but do not act. Knowledge is there but without endurance. Faith they have, but no conviction. Men are here, but without brains. A crowd here is, but not a single soul agreeable to one's heart. People come here simply to go away. They acknowledge the truth, then deny it and make things lawful and unlawful at their sweet will. Is your religion a sensual delight?

Ḥasan al-Baṣrī[46]

You have consented to serving your lower selves and pursuing your passions and natural inclinations. You work hard to satisfy and satiate your lower selves in this world, although this is something you will never achieve.

You keep to this state, hour after hour, day after day, and year after year, until you find that death has suddenly come to you and you cannot escape from its grip.

Al-Jīlānī[47]

Whoever elevates his vision above tangible and imagined things and his intentions above blameworthy desires, God has raised him to the horizons of the angels close to Him.

While whoever restricts his vision to tangible things and his aspirations to the passions the beasts share with him, God will reduce him to the lowest ranks.

Al-Ghazālī[48]

Do not let the self in you rush madly after inordinate desires, because it will drive you to the path of wickedness and vice, or oppression and tyranny.

ʿAlī ibn Abī Ṭālib[49]

Allah does not ask man to suppress his desires because He knows that it is not possible for him to do so. He simply asks man to control his desires and not let them control him.

Sayyid Quṭb[50]

Where part of you goes the rest will follow – given time.
You call yourself a teacher; therefore learn.[51]

Rābiʿa al-ʿAdawiyya[52]

5

Sincerity

ʿAbdullāh ibn Masʿūd (may Allah be well pleased with him) narrated that the Messenger of Allah (peace be upon him) said:

> "Sincerity is to purify the action from seeking the attention of the people."[53]

Ḥadīth

O you who worship without having your hearts present! The likeness of you is as the likeness of a donkey that has had its eyes blindfolded while turning the mill. It thinks it has walked many miles, when in fact it has not left its place.

Al-Jīlānī[54]

It is truly said that sincerity is the purification of action from the consideration of created beings. And it is also well said that sincerity means to guard against giving attention to the opinions of others.

Al-Qushayrī[55]

The slave is protected only through sincerity and self-control.

Abū Madyan[56]

For the sound heart there is nothing sweeter or more delightful than the sweetness of faith, which includes servitude to, love for and sincerity towards Allah.

Ibn Taymiyya[57]

Sincerity is the believer's plot of land, while his deeds are its surrounding walls. The walls are subject to alteration and change, but not so the ground. Only upon dutiful devotion can a building be firmly based.[58]

Al-Jīlānī[59]

The minimum of truthfulness requires that what one is in private and in public be the same.

Al-Qushayrī[60]

6

Patience

Abū Sa'īd al-Khudrī (may Allah be well pleased with him) said that the Messenger of Allah (peace be upon him) said:

"There is no gift better or wider than patience."[61]

Ḥadīth

Allah knows full well that I am innocent. But if despite innocence I make a confession, who is going to doubt the truth of the allegation? And if I deny the allegation, who is going to believe? My condition is like that of Joseph's father who declared that patience is the best course.

'Ā'isha[62]

Make patience your provision, satisfaction your mount and the truth your goal and objective.

Abū Madyan[63]

All good things are obtainable through patience.

Al-Jīlānī[64]

Patience primarily means not to complain to anyone other than Allah, not to let the heart feel angry with one's fate and not to let the organs express wrath, sorrow, grief and the like in a forbidden way.

Ibn Qayyim al-Jawziyya[65]

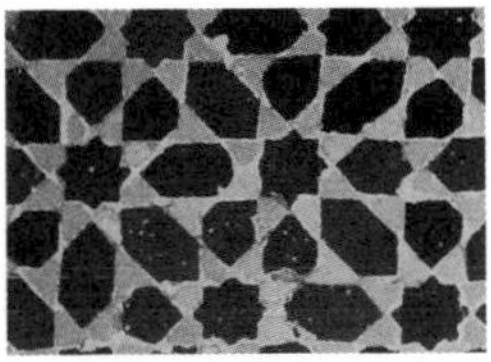

II
The Self and God

1

Freedom and Servitude

ʿAbdullāh ibn ʿAmr ibn al-ʿĀṣ (may Allah be well pleased with him) narrated that he heard Allah's Messenger (peace be upon him) say:

> "Verily, the hearts of all the sons of Adam are between the two fingers of the Compassionate Lord, as one heart. He turns it in any (direction) He likes."
> Then Allah's Messenger (peace be upon him) said:
> "O Allah, the Turner of hearts, turn our hearts to obedience to You."[66]

Ḥadīth

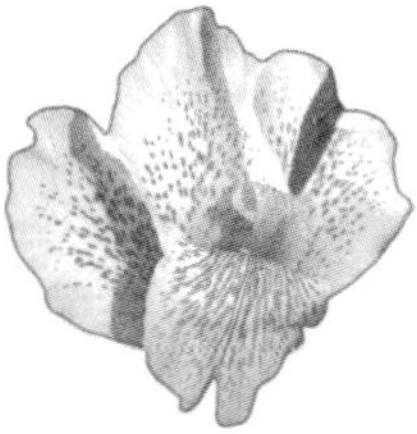

God indeed created mankind for whatever His established knowledge desired in creating it and for whatever its destiny should be.

Imām Shāfiʿī[67]

When the human heart releases itself from believing in anything but the one Truth, the Truth of Allah, and upholds this everlasting Truth, it liberates itself from all the shackles, false ideas, evil desires, fear from earthly power and from the confusions that mislead in this life.

Sayyid Quṭb[68]

Man can only attain perfection by being a true slave to Allah. The more his servitude increases the more perfect he becomes and the higher he rises in status. Whoever imagines that a person could release himself from this servitude in some way or another or that releasing oneself from it is better and more perfect, is one of the most ignorant of people and one of the furthest astray.

Ibn Taymiyya[69]

Freedom means that the servant is not slave to created beings and that things and events do not exercise control over him.

Al-Qushayrī[70]

No one attains true freedom as long as he remains under the influence of the slightest portion of his ego.

Abū Madyan[71]

O Young Man, the religion in the sight of Allah is Islam and the reality of Islam is surrender. You have to achieve Islam first and then fulfil surrender. Purify yourself through surrender. Surrender yourself to your Lord and be satisfied with His management of your affairs. Give up your will and accept the destiny your Lord has decreed. Consider all that destiny brings to you as acceptable. Your Lord knows you better than you know yourself, accept His word with certitude. Receive His commandments and prohibitions with total acceptance. Receive His religion with all of your heart and make it your inner and outer cover. Take full advantage of your life before the advent of a "Day from Allah that cannot be turned back from"[72] which is the Day of Resurrection.

Al-Jīlānī[73]

Know that the reality of freedom is the perfection of servitude.[74]

Al-Qushayrī[75]

2

Closeness to Allah

Narrated Abū Hurayra (may Allah be well pleased with him): "The Messenger of Allah (peace be upon him) said:

> "Allah says: 'I am in accordance with the thoughts of My slave about Me; and I am with him when he remembers Me. If he remembers Me in his heart, I also remember him in My heart. If he remembers Me in a gathering, I remember him in a more exalted gathering. If he draws near Me by the span of a hand, I draw near him by an arm's length. If he draws near Me by an arm's length, I draw near him by two arm lengths. If he walks towards Me, I go to him running.' "[76]

Ḥadīth

Whoever would like to know his place with God, let him look at God's place with him.

Al-Qushayrī[77]

Anyone who seeks Allah (Almighty and Glorious is He) will surely find Him.

Al-Jīlānī[78]

Woe unto you! How can you wish nearness of Allah when prohibited things have infiltrated your body through your food and drink, when your lower self is in control of you, when your passion is guiding you, when you are inclined toward lustful desires and pleasures, and when the fire of your natural inclination is burning out your fear of Allah and your religion?

Al-Jīlānī[79]

O Lord, render You the best of my life at its close, the best of my deeds as the last, and the best of my days, the day of Your meeting.

Abū Bakr[80]

Whether one be slow or speedy, he that is a seeker will be a finder. Always apply yourself with bold hands to seeking, for search is an excellent guide on the way. Though you may be lame and limping and bent in figure and unmannerly, ever creep toward Him and be in quest of Him. Now by speech and now by silence and now by smelling, catch in every corner the scent of the King. Inquire by means of the sense of the mouth, and lay your ear on the four roads (of that which you seek). Whenever a sweet scent comes, smell in that direction. Whenever you are aware of kindness from someone it is possible you may find the way to the source of kindness. All those lovely things are from a deep sea, leave the part and keep thine eye upon the whole.[81]

Rūmī[82]

3

Remembrance

Abū Hurayra (may Allah be well pleased with him) narrated that the Messenger of Allah (peace be upon him) said that Allah said:

"My servant continues to draw near to Me by voluntary services so that I love him, and when I love him I become his hearing whereby he hears, and his sight whereby he sees, and his hands wherewith he seizes, and his feet wherewith he walks. And if he asks of Me I give him, and if he betakes himself to Me, I give him refuge."[83]

Ḥadīth

May God steal from you all that steals you from Him.

Rābiʿa al-ʿAdawiyya[84]

Remembrance of God is liberation from ignorance and forgetfulness through the permanent presence of the heart with the Truth.

Al-Iskandarī[85]

One of the special features of the practice of remembrance is that it has no assigned time.

Al-Qushayrī[86]

Listening to recitation is the perfume of the souls, the calmer of the hearts and the food of the spirit.

Al-Suyūṭī[87]

Prayer offers protection from something bad, namely shameful and unjust deeds, and helps one to achieve something good, namely remembrance of Allah. Achieving this good is more important than protecting oneself from that bad, for remembering Allah and worshipping Him with all one's heart is the ultimate aim, whereas protecting oneself from evil is just a means to an end.

Ibn Taymiyya[88]

Protect yourself from the misfortunes of corrupt imaginings that distract you from remembrance.

Ibn ʿArabī[89]

Invoking Allah is the light for the servant in this world, his grave, his resurrection and his assembling with others on the Day of Judgement.

Al-Iskandarī[90]

Whosoever observes what God has commanded and abstains from what God has forbidden is one who remembers God.

Al-Iskandarī[91]

4

Love

Mu'ādh (may Allah be well pleased with him) narrated that the Messenger of Allah (peace be upon him) reported these words directly from Allah the Most High:

> "My love belongs to those who love each other in Me, who experience intimacy in Me, who shower each other with goodness for My Sake and who visit each other joyfully for My sake."[92]

Ḥadīth

Whoever comes to taste the love of God can have no taste for the love of this world.

Abū Bakr al-Ṣiddīq[93]

Woe unto you! You claim to love Allah, yet with your hearts you devote yourselves to others. Because Majnūn was truly sincere in his love for Laylā, his heart would not notice anyone other than her. He came across some people one day and they asked him, "Where are you coming from?" "From being with Laylā," he said. Then they asked him, "Where do you intend to go now?" "To Laylā," he replied.[94]

Al-Jīlānī[95]

There is no complete happiness and total delight but in the love of Allah, and in practising the acts instructed by Him. This love is attained through the rejection of all others and this is the reality of Lā ilāha illal-Lāh.

Ibn Taymiyya[96]

Whoever loves Allah must follow the Messenger, believe in what he says, obey what he commands and emulate what he does. Whoever does this does what Allah loves and so Allah will love him.

Ibn Taymiyya[97]

God loves everyone and every action tracing the signs and sense of His names and attributes.

Ibn Qayyim al-Jawziyya[98]

5
Fear

Abū Saʿīd Al-Khudrī (may Allah be well pleased with him) narrated that the Messenger of Allah (peace be upon him) said to his companions:

> "A man from among the early people or those before you had said a word, i.e. Allah had blessed him with wealth and sons. When death approached him he asked his sons, "How was I being as a father?" They replied: "You were the best father." He said, "I didn't save or perform any good deeds for Allah. If Allah takes possession of me, He will punish me. So, look! When I am dead burn me until I become coal, then crush me well and scatter my ashes in the air on a stormy day." The Prophet (peace be upon him) said: "He took a covenant from his sons (and died). They did according to his will and spread his ashes in the air on a stormy day." Allah (SWT) said: "Be!" And there he was embodied before Him. Allah the Exalted asked him: "O my slave! What induced you to do what you did?" He replied: "It was Your fear (so that I may

not appear before You)." The Prophet (peace be upon him) added: "Allah, the Exalted rewarded him with His Mercy." The Prophet (peace be upon him) said a second time "Allah did not punish him."[99]

Ḥadīth

Call on God and you will be sheltered from all fear. Trust in Him and you will find happiness. But alas! Who knows how to give an ear to what I say? Who can grasp it's full meaning and etch it into his memory?

Al-Muqaddisī[100]

Let each bondsman look to himself and to whether he is closer to the wrongdoers or the God-fearing. And look to yourself after having seen the conduct of the righteous predecessors.[101] For despite the success they were granted they were among the fearful.

Al-Ghazālī[102]

Fear is a whip that urges and restrains, it urges (you) toward obedience and restrains (you) from disobedience.

Abū Madyan[103]

The Allah-fearing ones are those who fear Allah in their public and private lives and watch for him under all circumstances. Their hearts shiver in fear of Him by day and by night.

Al-Jīlānī[104]

The person of fear, it is said, is not a person who weeps and rubs his eyes. The person of fear is only he who abandons that for which he is afraid he will be punished.

Al-Qushayrī[105]

Every heart that has no fear (of Allah) is like a town without trees, or sheep without a shepherd. Such a town is nothing but ruins and such sheep are doomed to be food for the wolves.

Al-Jīlānī[106]

6

Repentance

On the authority of Anas (may Allah be well pleased with him) who said, "I heard the Messenger of Allah (peace be upon him) say:

> "Allah, Blessed and Most High, said: 'O Son of Adam, as long as you call upon Me and put your hope in Me, I have forgiven you for what you have done and I do not mind. O Son of Adam, if your sins were to reach the clouds of the sky and then you would seek My forgiveness, I would forgive you.
>
> O Son of Adam, if you were to come to Me with sins that are close to filling the earth and you would then meet Me without ascribing any partners with Me, I would certainly (also) bring to you forgiveness close to filling it (the Earth).'"[107]

Ḥadīth

Hark, do not act (so) henceforth, but take precaution, for through bounty, the Door of Repentance is open. From the quarter of the west the Door of Repentance is open to mankind till the Resurrection. Till the sun lifts up its head from the west that door is open, do not avert your face from it. By the Mercy (of God) Paradise has eight doors, one of those eight doors is repentance. O Son! All the others are sometimes open, sometimes shut and never is the Door of Repentance but open. Come seize the opportunity, the door is open, carry your baggage there at once despite the envious (devil).

Rūmī[108]

"It puzzles me that a man should perish when he possesses the means to save himself." Asked to explain, he said, "The prayer for forgiveness."

ʿAlī ibn Abī Ṭālib[109]

May Allah pardon us, our stumbling! Treacherous the hand of Fortune proved, the nights we laughed and loved.

Fate flatters to deceive, rejoices but to grieve, a serpent in the bloom – we gather to our doom.[110]

Ibn ʿAbdūn[111]

In the Name of God I begin, with all my respect, and all praise belongs to God, for my strength and maturity.

I seek the forgiveness of God, our Lord and Creator, for all mankind and for the evils of my (soul's) turmoil.

I seek the forgiveness of God, motivator of the heavenly spheres in the darkness, for our failure to thank Him enough for His bounty.

I seek the forgiveness of God, the Saviour of one who seeks His aid, whenever he suffers misfortune or calamity.

I seek the forgiveness of God, Forgiver of the sins of one, who comes to Him broken, humiliated and full of remorse.

I seek the forgiveness of God, concealer of the faults of the morally deficient, and their Saviour from adversity.

I seek the forgiveness of God for my secret thoughts and overt acts, for the fickleness of my heart and for the smile upon my lips.

I seek the forgiveness of God for my speech and my behaviour, for my evil character, type and nature.

I seek the forgiveness of God, for my words and deeds, for my vain strivings, and the exhaustion of my abilities.

I seek the forgiveness of God, for my ignorance and transgressions, for the greatest of my conscious sins, and the minor ones I have committed.

I seek the forgiveness of God, for what my hand has wrought, for my errors and (the sins) toward which I was inclined.

I seek the forgiveness of God, for that which my hand did not earn, for that which I earned upon attaining adulthood.

I seek the forgiveness of God for saying 'I' and 'Me', (for saying) 'Belonging to me' and 'Mine', and for my suspicions and my (limited) understanding.

I seek the forgiveness of God, for that which I did not know, for that which I knew, and for that which I wrote by pen.

I seek the forgiveness of God, for my sleep, my lethargy, and my wakefulness, and for that which has maintained me (in life).

I seek the forgiveness of God, during the day, its night, and its morrow, before it is created from nothingness.

I seek the forgiveness of God, for that which occurred during my youth, and for my disagreements with the aged and the mature.

I seek the forgiveness of God, as often as I have feared what he has bestowed, and (as often as) the clouds have rained on the plains and the hills.

I seek the forgiveness of God, as often as the number of pilgrims, going towards land characterized by purity and sanctity.

I seek the forgiveness of God, as often as the breaking of dawn, and as often as the doves coo their songs in the branches.

I seek the forgiveness of God, as often as the number of letters (in the Qur'ān), and multiplicity of Qur'ānic verses and aphorisms recited during invocation.

I seek the forgiveness of God, as often as the number of riding animals, worlds beyond the horizons, and landmarks in the earth.

I seek the forgiveness of God, as often as the number of plants and sheep on the land, and (the amount of bounty) in the sea.

I seek the forgiveness of God, as often as the number of heavenly bodies, encompassed by knowledge, and for everything that is apparent and hidden.

I seek the forgiveness of God, as often as the number of (grains of) sand, and the (amount of) rain that falls continuously on the earth.

I seek the forgiveness of God, as often as the number of created things, of human beings and jinn, of Arabs and non-Arabs.

I seek the forgiveness of God, as often as the number of thoughts in the breasts of those endowed with trust, authority and wisdom.

I seek the forgiveness of God, all Majesty be to God, our Creator, Creator of mankind and the one who brought us forth from nothingness.

I seek the forgiveness of God, all Majesty be to God, Who provided for us, prior to physical existence, and Who apportions all shares (of worldly destiny).

I seek the forgiveness of God, Whose bounties are without number, the All-Encompassing, the Most Excellent, (The One) noted for generosity.

I seek the forgiveness of God, all Majesty be to God, Who gathers us in (at death), the Annihilator of centuries, and Annihilator of all nations.

I seek the forgiveness of God, all Majesty be to God, Who resurrects us after death, and Who gives life to decaying bones.

I seek the forgiveness of God, innumerable times, as often as the known species and breaths of life.

I seek the forgiveness of God, on Him be praises without number, (for) He causes Himself to be praised pre-eternally.

I seek the forgiveness of God, the Forgiver of sins, Who, whenever the slave disobeys, forgives him with indulgence and generosity.

So forgive the greatest of my transgressions, and (on) the Day of Judgement, when my feet are about to stumble.

Then may blessings be on the Chosen one from Mudar, the Best of Mankind[112], amongst those who weep or smile.

And may his family and companions be preserved, by our Lord, along with all (their) companions.

Abū Madyan[113]

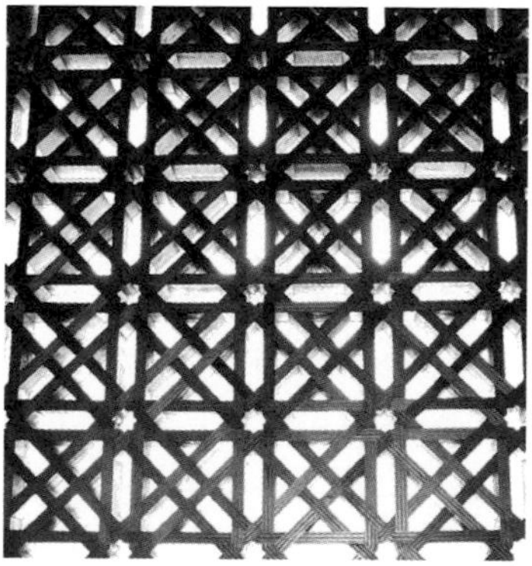

7

Humility

Abū Hurayra (may Allah be well pleased with him) reported the Messenger of Allah (peace be upon him) as saying:

> "Charity does not in any way decrease wealth and the servant who forgives Allah adds to his respect, and the one who shows humility, Allah elevates him in the estimation (of the people)."[114]
>
> *Ḥadīth*

He who exalts his neck with pride is girt with foes on every side, Saʿdī lies, prostrate, free from care, none of the fallen ere make war.

Reflection first, speech last of all, the basement must precede the wall.

True that the art of making flowers I know, but shall I try it where real flowers grow?

A beauty I – but will my cheek look fair, when they with Canaan's[115] glory me compare?

Shaykh Saʿdī[116]

O You, who own so much property, forget about your property! Come and sit here, in the midst of the poor. Be humble in the presence of Allah and in their presence.

O You, who possess such a noble pedigree, forget about your pedigree and come here. The genuinely noble pedigree is devotion to righteousness.

Al-Jīlānī[117]

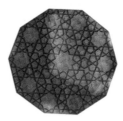

8

Gratitude

Al-Ibshīhī reported that the Messenger of Allah (peace be upon him) said:

> "He who does not thank for the little, does not thank for the abundant, and he who does not thank people, does not thank Allah. Talking about Allah's graces is an act of thanks."[118]
>
> *Ḥadīth*

What would be the value of all your good deeds in comparison to the smallest favour for which you are ungrateful?

Ibn Qayyim al-Jawziyya[119]

Return to us the nights that have been lost to us, and erase, by Your favour, that which has issued from us.

How much we have sinned, yet out of generosity You forgive; how much we have erred, yet we'll still hope for Your good pardon!

Nothing but You have I, You are the recourse of my sorrow, I have been ignorant and possess nothing but Your indulgence.

Not for a single day have I turned toward anyone but You, for in the entire world I own nothing but Your favour.

How much respect I display in (my) love (for You); no friendship do I hope for other than Your affection.

Were I to have a thousand tongues with which to express thanks to You, I would not stop thanking You a single day.

Abū Madyan[120]

When few blessings come your way do not drive them away with thanklessness.

ʿAlī ibn Abī Ṭālib[121]

When the servant witnesses the favours of Allah, he realises that his good deeds are nothing in comparison to them. This is because no one can number Allah's favours, and the smallest one amongst them exceeds all the servant's good deeds. Therefore, the servant always has to contemplate Allah's right of gratitude upon him.

Ibn Qayyim al-Jawziyya[122]

Cloud and wind and sun and sky labour all harmoniously, that while they you with food supply you may not eat unthankfully. Since all are busy and intent for you, justice forbids that you a rebel be.

Shaykh Saʿdī[123]

III
The *S*elf and *M*ankind

1

Unity

On the authority of Abū Ḥamza Anas ibn Mālik, the servant of the Messenger of Allah (May Allah be well pleased with him), from the Prophet (peace be upon him), who said:

> "None of you truly believes until he loves for his brother what he loves for himself."[124]

Ḥadīth

The population of the city came out to greet the members of our party and on all sides greetings and questions were exchanged. But not a soul greeted me as there was none known to me. I was so affected by my loneliness that I could not restrain my tears and wept bitterly. Until one of the pilgrims realised the cause of my distress, and coming up to me greeted me kindly and continued to entertain me with friendly talk until I entered the city.[125]

Ibn Baṭṭūṭa[126]

Once you have sensed that your brother is in need of something go offer it to him at once. Do not wait for him to come to ask for it.[127]

Al-Ghazālī[128]

Group feeling is necessary to the Muslim community. Its existence enables the community to fulfil what God expects of it.

Ibn Khaldūn[129]

You should know that one of the great principles of this religion is the bringing of Muslim hearts together and unifying their call.

Ibn Taymiyya[130]

Do not non-cooperate with each other and hold no grudge of jealousy.

Abū Bakr[131]

If you expect the blessings of God be kind to His people.

Abū Bakr[132]

Nothing is this world is worth discord between brothers.

Ibn al- Ḥusayn al-Sulamī[133]

O Lord, God! Unify the nation of Muḥammad.[134]

ʿUthmān[135]

2

Social and Political Affairs

Mu ʿāwiya (may Allah be well pleased with him) narrated that the Messenger of Allah (peace be upon him) said:

> "Any *Umma* (community) which does not apply justice, and the weak do not fully get their rights from the powerful, will never be sanctified."[136]

Ḥadīth

Islam cannot fulfil its role except by taking concrete form in a society, rather than in a nation. For man does not listen, especially in this age, to abstract theory, that is not materialised in a living form.

Sayyid Quṭb[137]

It is necessary for men to both associate with each other and to behave like citizens. This is obvious. It also follows that it is necessary to the life and survival of mankind that there should be co-operation between them, which can only be realised through a common transaction of business, in addition to all the other means, which secure the same purpose. This transaction requires a code of law and just regulation, which in their turn call for a lawgiver and regulator.

Ibn Sīnā[138]

The man that wants to superimpose his own ideas over the *Sharīʿa* in the garb of political expediency, really claims that the guidance vouchsafed to man by God is imperfect and incomplete.

Ibn al-Jawzī[139]

Truth is a trust, falsehood treason. The weak among you shall be strong with me until, God willing, his rights have been vindicated. And the strong among you shall be weak with me till, if the Lord wills, I have taken what is due from him. Obey me as long as I obey Allah and His Prophet. When I disobey Him and His Prophet, then obey me not.[140]

Abū Bakr[141]

I must set out on a journey to make sure that people's affairs are being put right, because within the realm dwell many defenceless persons that cannot come to me. I must tour the realm to observe the revenue officers and enquire about their characters, and I must satisfy the petitions of the needy. It will be the best-spent year in all of my life.[142]

ʿUmar ibn al-Khaṭṭāb[143]

Verily, God has entrusted the charge of administration to me. I have not accepted this responsibility for the sake of riches or sensual delights, for God has already favoured me with a fortune that only a few can boast of. For I fully realise the grave responsibility of the charge entrusted to me. I have taken upon myself this obligation with a great deal of anxiety and heart searching.

I know I will be called upon to render the account in the presence of God, when claimants and defendants will be present to argue their cases on the Day of Requital, a Burdensome Day indeed, save for those on whom Allah showers His mercy and whom He protects from the grievous ordeal. I bid you to be cautious and God fearing in all the affairs of the state committed to your charge and ask you to fulfil your obligations, perform that which has been ordained by God and desist from the acts prohibited by *Sharīʿa*. You ought to keep an eye upon yourself and your actions, be cautious of the acts that unite you with Allah on the one hand and your liegemen on the other. You are aware that salvation and safety lie in complete submission to the Almighty, and the ultimate goal of all endeavours should be, by the same token, to make preparations for success on the Appointed Day. If you will you might take a lesson from the happenings around you. Only then can I drive home the truth to you through my preaching.[144]

ʿUmar ibn ʿAbd al-ʿAzīz[145]

I commend you to God Almighty; He is the source of all good. Do the will of God for that is the way of peace. Beware of bloodshed; trust not in that, for spilt blood never sleeps. Seek to gain the hearts of thy subjects and watch over all their interests, for you are only appointed by God and by me to look after their good. Endeavour to gain the hearts of your emirs, your ministers and your nobles.

I have become as great as I am because I have won the hearts of men by gentleness and kindness. Never nourish ill feeling against any man for death spares none. Be prudent in your dealings with other men; God will not pardon unless they forgive you, but as to that which is between God and yourself, He will pardon the penitent for He is Gracious.[146]

Ṣalāḥ al-Dīn al-Ayyūbī[147]

I do not want to hear the nonsensical pleadings of your case. It is useless to prove your honesty and integrity as I am sending Muḥammad ibn Maslama for the purpose that you hand over half your assets to him. You are on the mainspring of riches and offer lame excuses when caught and accounted for. You are amassing wealth for your heirs, levelling the foundations of property through the help of your office. No doubt you are gathering the paraphernalia of condemnation, surely to be morsel of the Hellfire. And Salām.[148]

ʿUmar ibn al-Khaṭṭāb[149]

Oppressor!
Troubler of the poor!
How soon shall this, your mart be over?
What good will empire be to you?
Better your death than tyranny.

Shaykh Saʿdī[150]

3

Enjoining Good and Forbidding Evil

On the authority of Abū Saʿīd al-Khudrī (may Allah be well pleased with him) who said,

> "I heard the Messenger of Allah (peace be upon him) say: "Whoever of you sees an evil must change it with his hand. If he is unable to do so (he must change it) with his tongue. And if he is not able to do so (he must change it) with his heart and that is the slightest (effect of) faith."[151]

Ḥadīth

The walls of the religion of the Prophet (peace be upon him) have come tumbling down, they are crying out for help, for someone to rebuild it.

Al-Jīlānī[152]

There is nothing in our Islam of which we are ashamed or anxious about defending, there is nothing in it to be smuggled to the people with deception, nor do we muffle the loud truth, which it proclaims.

Sayyid Quṭb[153]

Enjoining good and prohibiting evil is the basic subject of religion. It is such a necessity for which all the Prophets were sent to the world. Had it been closed Prophethood would have been meaningless, religion lost, idleness reigned, ignorance spread and disturbance prevailed, dangers and calamities appeared and mankind destroyed.

Al-Ghazālī[154]

Do not forget yourself while preaching to others.

ʿUmar ibn al-Khaṭṭāb[155]

Their shoulders you shook when they parted, but they completely forsook you, when you went away.

Fine lessons you teach, but yourself do not school, grand sermons you preach, but remain still a fool.

How long will you whet other's swords on your stone? Continuing yet not to cut with your own.

Al-Mahdī[156]

4
Speech

Ibn ʿUmar (may Allah be well pleased with him) narrated that the Messenger of Allah (peace be upon him) said:

> "Verily, many a speech is enchantment and verily, many a poetry is sound sense."[157]

Ḥadīth

Silence is mannerly, so deem the wise but in the fitting time use language free.

Blindness of judgement lies in two things: to speak unwished, not speak unreasonable.

Shaykh Saʿdī[158]

Silence is security. That is the root of the matter. This can be a cause for recourse on occasions when keeping quiet is blameworthy. What is necessary is that one chooses speech or silence according to the Divine Law and the obligation of a Muslim to commend what is good and forbid what is evil. To say nothing at the proper time is a characteristic of true men, just as to speak at the proper occasion is one of the noblest of qualities.[159]

Al-Qushayrī[160]

Better who sits in nooks, deaf, speechless, idle, than he who knows not his own tongue to bridle.

Shaykh Saʿdī[161]

The dangers and harms of the tongue are many and there is no rescue from them except silence.

Al-Ghazālī[162]

A fool's mind is at the mercy of his tongue and a wise man's tongue is under the control of his mind.

ʿAlī ibn Abī Ṭālib[163]

One who talks too much makes the most mistakes.

ʿAlī ibn Abī Ṭālib[164]

You talk such a lot and yet you do so little. You must try to turn this around.

Al-Jīlānī[165]

When you speak take care to speak only from your own experience and your own state. You should not talk about what you have not lived.

Ibn al-Ḥusayn al-Sulamī[166]

You are crazy. You compose your speech from books and then deliver it. If you lost your written notes, what would you do? What if your books caught fire? Or if the lamp you use to read by, went out? If your jar broke and the ink spilled where would you find your flint, your tinderbox, your matches and your fuel? When someone acquires knowledge, puts it into practice and does so sincerely, his flint and his fuel come to be within his heart. A light from the light of Allah, Almighty and Glorious is He. He can then provide illumination for himself and others. Away with you, O sons of babble!

Al-Jīlānī[167]

Anyone who glories in the sound of his own voice let it be known to him that many of the birds have sweeter voices than he. And the sound of the flute is more exquisite and charming than the sound of his voice.

Ibn Ḥazm[168]

5
Friendship

Abū Mūsā (may Allah be well pleased with him) reported Allah's Messenger (peace be upon him) as saying:

> "The similitude of good company and of bad company is that of the owner of musk and of the one (ironsmith) blowing bellows. The owner of musk would either offer it to you free of charge or you would buy it from him, or you would smell its pleasant odour. And as far as the one who blows bellows is concerned, he would either burn your clothes or you shall have to smell its repugnant smell." [169]

Ḥadīth

Nothing you possess deserves to be more jealously guarded or vigilantly cherished than the friend that you have proved through thick and thin, whose ways you know, whose virtues you have tested, whose innermost thoughts are pure and whose attitude to you is one of frankness. He is the brother of your soul and the gateway to peace in your lifetime; his thoughts are an extension of yours and his mind the twin of yours.

Al-Jāḥiẓ[170]

If you were ever fortunate to come across a truthful person, stay close to him. If you were ever fortunate to come across one who has your remedy, stick always close to him. If you ever had the good fortune to come across one who guides you to what you have lost, stick always close to him. You may never get to know such people, for they are few and far between.

Al-Jīlānī[171]

If you wish to know whether those you mix and sit with increase or diminish your faith, religion and actions, compare your state with regards to good character, praiseworthy intentions, and resolution in performing acts of obedience and goodness, before and after their companionship.

Al-Ḥaddād[172]

Anyone who makes friends with a fool must be a fool himself.

Al-Jīlānī[173]

Loneliness is better than bad company.

Al-Jīlānī[174]

Avoid the friend who's parasitic
(Like certain particles enclitic)
And loves to be, like Amr, a ranger
Between compatriot and stranger.

Bad company is most contagious
As proof of its effect outrageous
The spear that in bad blood keeps dipping
Shows on its point with what it's dripping.[175]

Abū ʿAmr[176]

The man who obeys God the most is the best and most sincere friend of his own self, and the man who disobeys Him is his own worst and deadliest enemy.

ʿAlī ibn Abī Ṭālib[177]

6

Advice

On the authority of Abū Ruqayya Tamīm ibn Aws (may Allah be well pleased with him), the Messenger of Allah (peace be upon him) said:

> "The religion is sincerity." The people said, "To whom?" The Prophet replied, "To Allah and to His Book and to His Messenger and to the Leaders of the Muslims and to the common folk of the Muslims."[178]

Ḥadīth

He who is not impressed by sound advice lacks faith.

Abū Bakr[179]

A certain man caught a bird by guile and trap. The bird said, "O Noble Sir, you have eaten oxen and sheep, you have sacrificed many camels. They have never in the world sated you; neither shall my limbs sate you. Let me go that I may bestow on you three counsels that you may perceive whether I am wise or foolish. (I will give you) the first of these counsels on your hand, the second of them on your plastered roof and the third counsel I will give you on a tree. (Let me go) for you will become fortunate through these three counsels. (As for) that saying which is (to be said) on your hand, it is this: do not believe in absurdity from anyone."

When it had uttered the first grave counsel on his palm it became free and went (to perch) on the wall (of the man's house) and said, " The second is: do not grieve over what is past, when it has passed from you do not regret it."

After that it said to him, "In my body is concealed a solitary, large and precious pearl, ten darāhim[180] in weight. By your soul's truth as sure as you live, that jewel was the fortune and the luck of your children. You have missed the pearl for it was not your appointed lot, a pearl of which is not in existence."

Even as a woman big with child keeps wailing at the time of parturition, so the Khawāja began to cry out clamourously. The bird said to him, "Did I not admonish you saying, let there be no grief in you for what passed yesterday? Since it is passed and gone why are you grieving? Either you did not understand my counsel or you are deaf. And (as regards) the first counsel I gave you, do not from misguidance put any belief in an absurd statement: O Lion, I myself do not weigh ten darāhim, how should the weight of ten darāhim be within me?"

The Khawāja came back to himself and said, " Hark, disclose the third counsel." "Yes," said the bird, "you have made good use of those (former counsels) that I should tell the third counsel in vain."

To give counsel to a sleepy ignoramus is to scatter seed into nitrous soil. The rent of folly and ignorance does not admit of being patched up. Do not give the seed of wisdom to him, the fool, O Counsellor!

Rūmī[181]

O young man! Do not accuse anyone on behalf of your Creator. You are just as likely to be mistaken, as you are to be correct.

Al-Jīlānī[182]

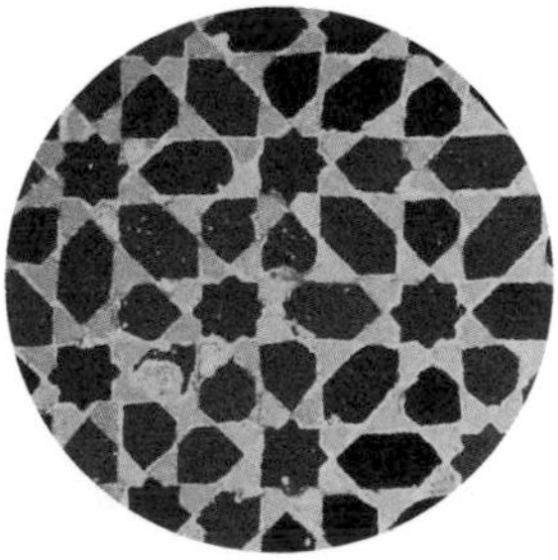

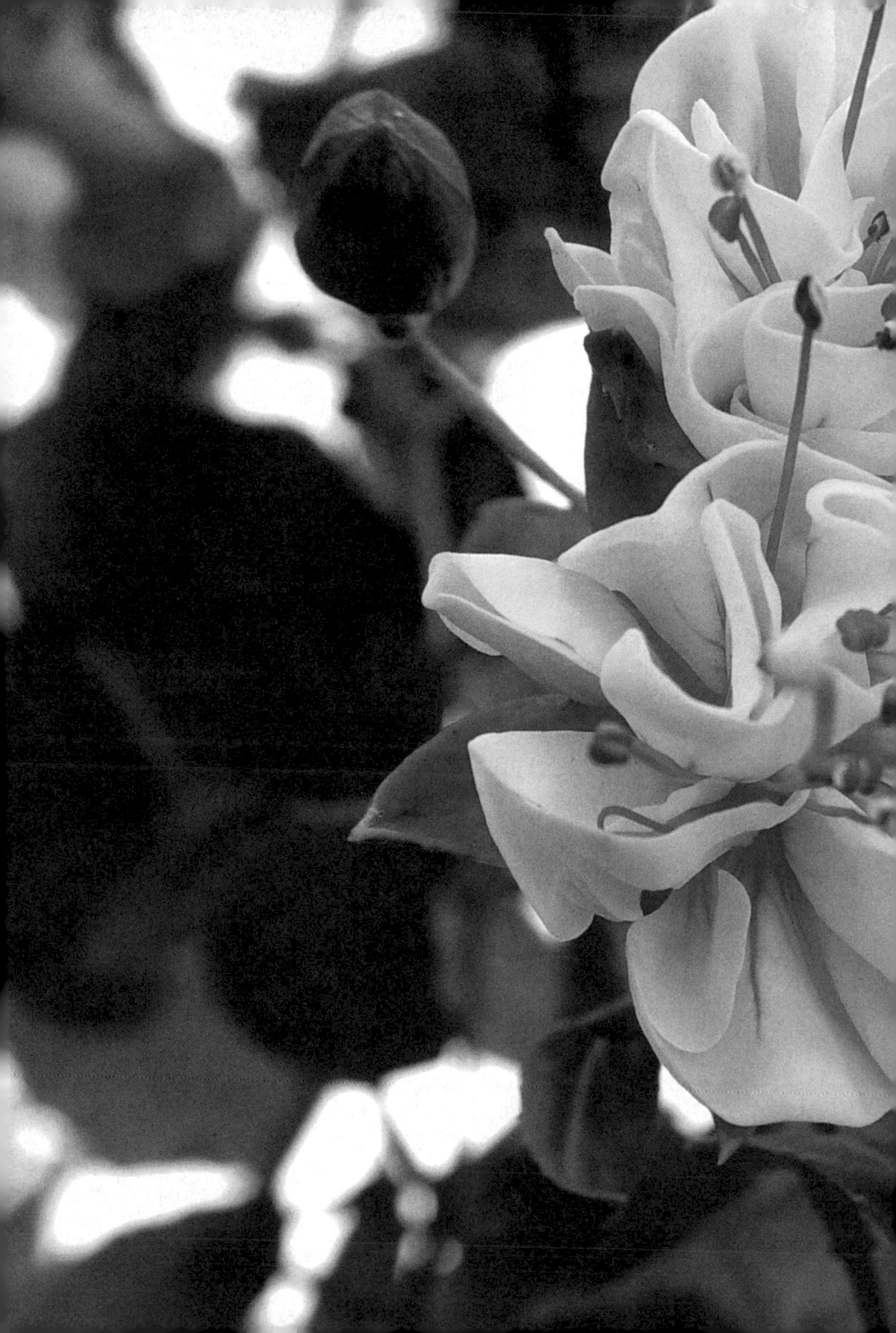

IV
The *Self* and the *World*

1

The World

On the authority of ibn ʿUmar (may Allah be well pleased with him) who said:

> "The Messenger of Allah (peace be upon him) took hold of my shoulder and said:
> "Be in this world as if you were a stranger or traveller along a path."[183]
>
> *Ḥadīth*

Is this world in its entirety anything more than that which we have experienced and seen?

In truth, by God we turned to face its attractions with our strivings and our revelling in our lives, yet not long was it before the world began to diminish us.

Condition after condition, attachment after attachment, until it defrauded and exhausted us.

So, how unworthy an abode is this world? How unworthy an abode is this world?

Muʿāwiya ibn Abī Sufyān[184]

Everything you are involved in, everything you are concerned about, all of it is nothing but a delusion wrapped up in yet another delusion.

Al-Jīlānī[185]

O you who delight in sumptuous splendour and magnificent chambers, you must have forgotten that this world is but a place for standing devotion. After sleeping on those luxurious beds, tomorrow you will descend to the narrow dark cell of the tomb. Your companions will be silent beings, but the energy in their silence is akin to speech. Ah, that a simple dress should be all your clothing and a spoonful or two should be all your food! Choose, like the spider, a modest dwelling and say to yourself: " Let us stay here and wait for death."

Al-Muqaddisī[186]

When will you put prayer before the business of your shop?
When will you put the Hereafter before your worldly interests?
When will you put the Creator before creatures?
When will you put the beggar before yourself?
When will you put obeying the commandments of Allah, observing His prohibitions and enduring with patience the tribulations that come from Him, before your passion and your habitual practice?
When will you put answering Him before answering His creatures?
Be sensible, you are in sheer illusion.

Al-Jīlānī[187]

Our abode in this world is transitory. Our life therein is but a loan. Our breaths are numbered and our indolence is manifest.

Abū Bakr[188]

This world is transient and a conveyance to transport us to another place. It is not a place where one should feel happy and pleased. The through-fare of our life will forsake us at a turning point. It is not a path to remain with us permanently.

Al-Nawawī[189]

Beware that this world is not made for you to live forever; you will have to change it for the hereafter.

ʿAli ibn Abī Ṭālib[190]

Know that Hope is the deaf man that has often heard of dying, but has not heard of his own death or regarded his own demise. The blind man is Greed; he sees other people's faults, hair by hair and tells them from street to street. But his blind eyes do not perceive one mote of his own faults, albeit he is a faultfinder.

The naked man is afraid that his skirt will be cut off, how should they cut off the skirt of a naked man?

The worldly man is destitute and terrified; he possesses nothing, yet he has dread of thieves. Bare he came and naked he goes and all the while his heart is bleeding with anxiety on account of the thief.

At the hour of death, when a hundred lamentations are beside him, his spirit begins to laugh at its own fear.
At that moment, the rich man knows that he has no gold and the keen-witted knows that he is devoid of talent.

Rūmī[191]

The world, my brother, will abide with none; by the world's Maker, let your heart be won.

Rely not, nor repose on this world's gain, for many a son like you has she reared or slain.

What matters, when spirit seeks to fly, if on a throne or on bare earth we die?

Shaykh Saʿdī[192]

Yesterday is past and gone with everything it contained to be a witness for and against you. As for tomorrow, you do not know if you will survive till then or not. You are simply the son of your today.

Al-Jīlānī[193]

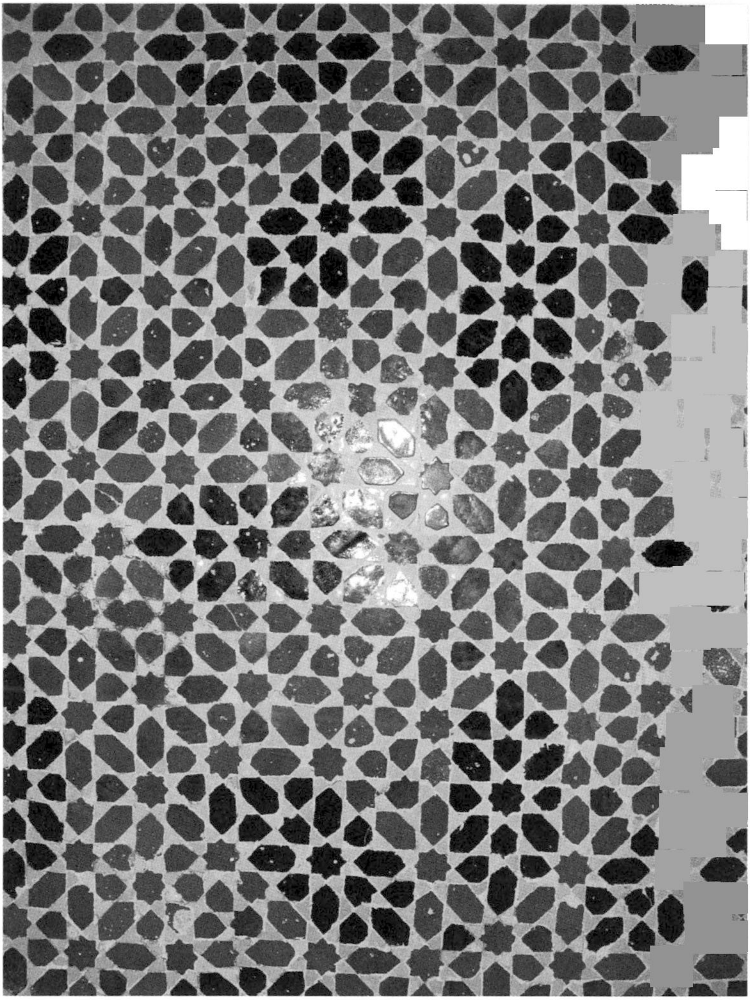

2

Actions

On the authority of Abū Dharr al-Ghifārī (may Allah be well pleased with him), from the Messenger of Allah (peace be upon him), among the sayings he relates from his Lord, is that He said:

"O My servants, I have forbidden wrongdoing for Myself, and have made it forbidden for you, therefore, do not wrong one another.

O My servants, all of you are lost except for those whom I have guided, therefore, seek guidance from Me and I shall guide you.

O My servants, all of you are hungry except for those whom I have fed, therefore, seek food from Me and I will feed you.

O My servants, all of you are naked except for those whom I have clothed, therefore, seek clothing from Me and I will clothe you.

O My servants, you sin by night and by day and I forgive all sins, therefore, seek forgiveness from Me and I will forgive you.

O My servants, you will not be able to harm Me, so as to bring any benefit to Me.

O My servants, if the first and the last of you and the human and the jinn of you were as pious as the most pious heart of anyone among you, it would not add anything to My dominion.

O My servants, if the first and the last of you, and the human and the jinn of you were as wicked as the wickedest heart of anyone among you, it would not decrease anything of My dominion.

O My servants, if the first and the last of you, the human and the jinn of you were to gather together on the land and all asked of Me, and if I were to give everyone of them what they asked, that would not decrease what I have any more than a needle decreases what is in the ocean when it is put into it.

O My servants, it is but your deeds that I reckon for you. Then I recompense you for them. The one who finds good is to give praises to Allah, the one who finds other than this should not blame anyone but himself."[194]

Ḥadīth

O King![195] We were uncivilised people, worshipping idols, eating corpses, committing abominations, breaking natural ties, inhospitable to our guests, and the strong devoured the weak. God has sent us His Messenger, a man whose noble roots, his truth, trustworthiness, honesty and clemency we know. He urged us to acknowledge God's unity and worship Him alone and renounce the stones and images that our ancestors and we formerly worshipped. He commanded us to speak the truth, to fulfil our commitments and be hospitable and mindful of kinship ties. He ordered us to refrain from crimes, blood shedding, committing abominations, telling lies, devouring the property of orphans and from vilifying chaste women. He taught us to be prayerful to God, to be charitable and assume a moderation in living.

Jaʿfar ibn Abī Ṭālib[196]

The path of the people of faith comprises knowledge of the truth and adherence to it in their conduct.

Ibn Kathīr[197]

What would be the benefit of the purity of the limbs and organs when combined with impurity of the heart? Purify your limbs and organs with the *Sunnah* and your heart with putting the Qur'ān into practice. Protect your heart so that your limbs and organs will be protected. Every vessel exudes its own contents! Whatever is in your heart will ooze out to your limbs and organs.

Al-Jīlānī[198]

As it is incumbent upon you to excel in everything that you do for the sake of God, such as good works and devotion, it is likewise incumbent upon you to excel in abstaining from evil, forbidden and doubtful things, and from cravings – all for the sake of God. Excellence in abstention is also to avoid situations in which one may lapse and to avoid the company of such kind of people that are likely to drag one along with them. Know this well! All success is from Allah!

Al-Ḥaddād[199]

The man who is either unable or lacks the energy to perform all the possible kinds of good works should not abandon them all, but should do whatever he finds easy and accessible. For goodness attracts goodness, the small attracts the great and a little invites plenty.

Al-Ḥaddād[200]

Steadfastness, continuing straight ahead without deviation, is a level that contains the perfection and completion of everything.

Al-Qushayrī[201]

People of realisation, gnosis, clear vision and certitude give precedence to excellence (*iḥsān*) in acting over the act itself. For the outward form of the acts, whether ritual prayer, fasting, recitation or invocation of God, will be nothing but hardship and toil of no benefit in the absence of thoroughness and excellence in performance, perfection of the inner dimensions, reverence before God, humility, submission, attention and the courtesy of behaviour that befits that Holy Sublime and august presence of God.

Al-Ḥaddād[202]

Just as a multitude of actions give rise to a strong and persistent habit, constant separation from it necessitates the weakness of the habit.

Al-Rāzī[203]

The goal is the straight path that leads the one who follows it to God. But there is not one of God's commandments without two ways of approach to the Devil: one by deficiency, the other by excess. And it makes no difference which of the two errors overtakes the servant. They appear in his heart as equals.

Ibn Qayyim al-Jawziyya[204]

The best form of devotion to God is not to make a show of it.

ʿAlī ibn Abī Ṭālib[205]

O People! Judge yourselves before you are judged and take account of your actions before you are asked to submit your account for them. Repent while there is still time at your disposal and submit to His orders before death ends all possibilities of improvement.

ʿAlī ibn Abī Ṭālib[206]

3
Provisions

Narrated Abū Wāqid al-Laythī (may Allah be well pleased with him), "We used to visit the Messenger of Allah (peace be upon him) to hear anything revealed to him. One day he said to us:

> "Allah said: 'Verily, We have bestowed (the believers) with fortune in order to offer prayers and pay charity. But if the son of Adam had one valley of money he would wish for the second. If he had two valleys, he would wish for the third. So nothing except soil can fill up the belly of the son of Adam. But Allah will forgive the one who repents to Him.' "[207]

Ḥadīth

In this fleeting world, His many manifestations of generosity and bounty include and encompass all human beings. He gave them ears, eyes and hearts and singled them out for possessing reason, which makes it possible for them to distinguish between truth and falsehood and to recognise what is useful and what is harmful.

Al-Ṭabarī[208]

Everything you seem to possess is merely on loan to you. Whether it be your youth, your good health, your leisure, your affluence, your poverty or your life itself, it is with you as a loan. So you had better take care of it.

Al-Jīlānī[209]

It is impossible to lay hands on that which is not predestined for us, and that which is predestined for us will reach us wherever we are.

Shaykh Saʿdī[210]

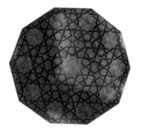

On him, He will bestow an ample provision whence he expect it not.

Ḥāfiẓ[211]

O seeker of the gold and silver coin, they are nothing! They are both in the hand of Allah so do not try to get them from creatures.

Al-Jīlānī[212]

4
Work

Narrated by Al-Miqdām (may Allah be well pleased with him), "The Messenger of Allah (peace be upon him) said:

> 'Nobody has ever eaten a better meal than that which one has earned by working with his own hands. The Prophet of Allah, Dā'ūd (upon him be peace), used to eat from the earnings of his manual labour.' "[213]

Ḥadīth

Woe unto you? Are you not embarrassed in the presence of Allah? You give up the effort to earn your living and go begging from other people. Earning is a starting point and absolute trust is a final stage, so I do not see you having either a beginning or an end.

Al-Jīlānī[214]

None of you should slacken in seeking His bounty, while saying "Please God provide for me," while you know the sky does not rain gold or silver.

ʿUmar ibn al-Khaṭṭāb[215]

Do not be idle but work in this world until you reach the definite state of trust in Allah.

Ibn al-Ḥusayn al-Sulamī[216]

When people no longer do business to make a living, the business of civilisation slumps and everything decays.

Ibn Khaldūn[217]

Civilisation and its well being, as well as business prosperity, depend on productivity and people's efforts in all directions in their own interest and profit.

Ibn Khaldūn[218]

5

Hardship

Al-Zuhrī said that ʿUrwa narrated that ʿĀ'isha (may Allah be well pleased with her) said, "The Messenger of Allah (peace be upon him) said:

> "Whenever a catastrophe happens to a Muslim, Allah will expiate his sins by it, even if a thorn pricks him."[219]
>
> *Ḥadīth*

Know that since God created human beings and brought them out of nothingness into existence they have not stopped being travellers. They have no resting place from their journey except in the Garden or the Fire...Every rational person must know that the journey is based upon toil and the hardships of life, on afflictions and tests and the acceptance of dangers and very great terrors. It is not possible for the traveller to find in this journey unimpaired comfort, security and bliss.

Ibn ʿArabī[220]

Know that those who demand from the world the needs of only one day have fewer troubles and worries than those who demand the needs of a week. While those who seek a month's needs have fewer worries than those who seek the needs of a year.

Al-Ḥaddād[221]

Worldly pleasures are not pure; they are mixed with pain and loss.

Imām Fakhr al-Dīn al-Rāzī[222]

The believer loves Allah even if He tests him with afflictions, even if He reduces his share of food, drink, clothing, social prestige and well being and drives creatures away from him. He does not run away from His door, but instead sleeps at it, taking its doorstep as his pillow, and he does not feel alienated from Him. He does not object to Him should He give blessings to others and deprive him. If He grants him blessings he offers thanks to Him and if He withholds things from him, he endures that with patience. His aim is not achieving blessings but his goal is seeing Him, nearing Him and entering into His presence.

Al-Jīlānī[223]

No misfortune will ever descend upon any of the followers of God's religion for which there is no guidance in the Book of God to indicate the right way.

Imām Shāfiʿī[224]

6

Death

Narrated by Abū Hurayra (may Allah be well pleased with him):

> "Allah's Messenger (peace be upon him) said that Allah the Exalted observed:
> 'If My slave loves meeting Me, I love meeting him. If he dislikes to meet Me, I too hate to meet him.' " [225]

Ḥadīth

O People, die before you die! Remember death frequently and prepare for its arrival and then you will have died before you die.

Al-Jīlānī[226]

Now, it behoves him for whom death is his destruction, the earth his bed, the worm his intimate, Munkar and Nakīr[227] his companions, the tomb his abode and the belly of the earth his resting place, the rising of his tryst and Heaven or Hell his destiny, that he should harbour no thought or recollection but death. No preparedness or plan should he have save for it, and his every expectation, concern, energy, waiting and anticipation should be for its sake alone. It is right that he should count himself among the dead and see himself as one of the people of the graves. For all that comes is certainly near, the distant is what never comes.

Al-Ghazālī[228]

Be prepared for the fast passage, because here you are destined for a short stay. Always be ready for death for you are living under its shadow.

ʿAlī ibn Abī Ṭālib[229]

O unfortunate one! Let death occupy your thoughts, for the voyage is urging you ever forward, while all the time you are in heedlessness of your own self.

Al-Ghazālī[230]

The duration of your life is but one breath. Take care that you master it and that it does not master you.

Abū Madyan[231]

Life is short, time is precious, death is near and the distance to travel is great, while the moment of standing before God to account for everything, however seemingly insignificant, is daunting and difficult.

Al-Ḥaddād[232]

Hour after hour, day after day, month after month and year after year, time goes by and death will come to you sooner or later, for you are powerless to escape it. Death has you under its constant surveillance, but you do not have a clue. You are too absentminded to notice, yet it is standing there staring you straight in the face. The moment is now very near at hand when one of you will be left abandoned in a field, namely, the field of the consequences you have earned and the life you have led.

Al-Jīlānī[233]

If this heedless man would but think and come to realise that death has no fixed time as to youth, middle age or decrepitude, and that it does not know winter from summer, autumn from spring or day from night, his awareness would be greater and he would busy himself with preparing for it. But ignorance of these matters combined with the love of this world invites man to prolong his hopes and to neglect any consideration of the proximity of death. Always does he think that death is ahead of him, but does not reckon upon its befalling him and that before long he will tumble into it. Constantly does he imagine that he will follow funeral corteges and never imagine that his own cortege will someday be followed.

Al-Ghazālī[234]

For a long time I have been thinking about death. I had certain dear friends, as closely bound to me by the bonds of sincere affection, as the soul is bound to the body. After they died some of them appeared in my dreams, others did not. While one of the latter was still alive, we had each promised to visit the other in a dream after we had died and if at all possible. But I have not seen him at all since he preceded me into the other world. I do not know whether he has forgotten or has been otherwise engaged.

Ibn Ḥazm[235]

There is no force to counter death. Whichever way you face and however you twist and turn, it is both the leader in front of you and the follower behind you.

Al-Jīlānī[236]

Death's hand has struck the signal drum;
Eyes! Now obey your parting knell!
Hands, wrists and arms, all members come,
And bid a mutual long farewell!
Hope's foe!
Death has seized me at last,
Once more my friends, before me move,
In folly has my time been passed.
May my regrets, your warning prove.

Shaykh Saʿdī[237]

When my life approaches its end, a moment of pain, shame and confusion, I will rise up, but with my eyes still lowered to the ground, in recognition of the error of my ways. Even if I do make every effort and drive from my eyes the sleep dust of indifference, I will still have to face the fact of my powerlessness and that I fear to be disappointed in my hope; all the more will I feel it, having slipped so seriously from grace in my past and finding myself tomorrow amongst penitents at the moment of death. What use can I glean from my knowledge and experience, when my eyes have no hope of ever seeing the light of day again? And so, let a salutary fear guide my steps from this day forward. Let us hurry, since haste is inherent in man!

Al-Muqaddisī[238]

Gird up your loins for death. Death shall surely meet you.
Do not be angry at death when it comes to your valley.[239]

ʿAlī ibn Abī Ṭālib[240]

"My physician has already looked at me and said: "I am the one who does as He wills." "[241]

Abū Bakr[242]

It is not wondrous that whoever smells the fragrance of Muḥammad's tomb will never smell another perfume.
Destiny hurt me with a bereavement so sad and so dark that had it fallen on the days, they would have turned into eternal nights.[243]

Fāṭima al-Zahra[244]

O Allah!
Grant us wakefulness before death,
Repentance before death,
Guidance before death,
Knowingness before death,
Doing business with You before death,
Returning to Your door before death,
And entering into the abode of Your nearness before death.
Amen.

Al-Jīlānī[245]

Profiles of those Quoted and Further Reading

Ibn ʿAbdūn
A 12th century litterateur from Evora in Andalusia. Died in 1134 CE.

ʿUmar Ibn ʿAbd al-ʿAzīz
Born in 61 AH, ʿUmar ibn ʿAbd al-ʿAzīz was the cousin of the Caliph Sulaymān ibn ʿAbd al-Malik and his mother, Umm ʿĀṣim, was the granddaughter of ʿUmar ibn al-Khaṭṭāb. He grew up amongst the privileged and elite of Muslim society, having access to all its resources, and also vulnerable to all its trappings.

As a young man he was appointed as governor to the city of Madīna and enjoyed the aristocratic lifestyle, indulging in various pleasures and pastimes. However, he was also known for his integrity and righteous character in public matters.

With the sudden illness of the Caliph ʿAbd al-Malik in 99 AH and the lack of a grown up son to succeed, ʿUmar ibn ʿAbd al-ʿAzīz was seen as the only possible successor to the throne. He was suddenly catapulted from governor of Madīna where he enjoyed a relatively stress-free position, to Caliph and defender of the entire Islamic world, becoming known in the process as ʿUmar.

II.

Although respected for his upright character and justice, no one could predict how seriously ʿUmar II would take his new role and how many important reforms he would seek to make. On his accession to the throne he began to make immediate changes to the abuse of power and resources widespread amongst state officials. Among other things, he:

- Deposited all jewellery and presents given to him on his accession in the state treasury and emancipated all slaves of the royal household.
- Set the stipends for state governors and officials, thus preventing abuse of the state treasury. Here he led by example and lived off a defined wage and would often arrive for the Friday prayer late because he had to wait for his only shirt to dry after being washed.
- Illegalised unpaid labour.
- Distributed land reserved for royal use amongst the poor.

ʿUmar II felt he had succeeded his own great-grandfather ʿUmar ibn al-Khaṭṭāb as Caliph, and thus set about to rule with the same level of integrity and justice. Through doing so he also created enemies, and after only two and a half years of ground-breaking leadership, he died in 101 AH under suspicious circumstances.

Muʿāwiya Ibn Abī Sufyān

Muʿāwiya ibn Abī Sufyān was born into a prominent Makka clan in the year 602 AC. His father was Abū Sufyān ibn Ḥarb, an important man of his tribe and bitter opponent of the Prophet Muḥammad (peace be upon him). Consequently, Muʿāwiya did not adopt Islam until the conquest of Makka in 630 CE, at which point he was made the Prophet's scribe and secretary.

During the Caliphate of Abū Bakr, Muʿāwiya was sent as part of the Islamic army to conquer Syria. At its conquest he was made governor over the city of Damascus and eventually, under ʿUmar ibn al-Khaṭṭāb, his governorship was extended to include the whole of the region. He served in this role for over twenty years, and set about extending the borders of the Muslim state through orchestrating raids into Asia Minor, Cyprus, Rhodes and the coast of Lycia.

At the murder of the third Caliph, ʿUthmān ibn ʿAffān, ʿAlī ibn Abī Ṭālib was elected leader. This change in leadership would prove to alter the direction of Muslim history and its circumstances brought about the first Muslim civil dispute.

As the strongest member of ʿUthmān's clan, the responsibility to call for the avenging of his murder fell on Muʿāwiya ibn Abī Sufyān, culminating in him refusing to acknowledge ʿAlī as rightful Caliph. This immediately threw the Muslim world into a dangerous and volatile situation that challenged people's loyalties and sense of justice. In 657 CE ʿAlī ibn Abī Ṭālib marched on Syria and the two sides engaged in the famous battle known as Battle of Ṣiffīn. Eventually a truce was agreed and arbitrators were chosen.

In 661 CE ʿAlī ibn Abī Ṭālib was murdered, thus bringing an end to the era of the *Khilāfat al-Rāshida* (The Rightly Guided Caliphate). With control over a vast amount of Muslim soil, it was felt Muʿāwiya was the best candidate for the Caliphate and he took the leadership. He immediately set about stabilising Muslim territory and sought to create unity across the various regions.

Muʿāwiya ibn Abī Sufyān died in the year 680 CE and was succeeded by his son Yazīd I.

Rābiʿa Al-ʿAdawiyya

Rābiʿa Al-ʿAdawiyya was born the fourth daughter into a poor but religious family between 95 and 99/717 in modern day Iraq. She remained with her parents and siblings until the tender age of eleven when, at the death of her father, her mother decided to move to Baṣra with her four children. During the difficult journey thieves robbed and killed her mother and the four girls were separated.

Rābiʿa found herself sold into slavery at an early age and had to undergo the various humiliations that women of her status were subjected to during those times. Eventually, she was given her freedom and chose to live an ascetic and celibate life in Baṣra.

Although she did not receive any education in the traditional sense, Rābiʿa Al-ʿAdawiyya's reputation as a profound thinker and orator grew across the region. She often spent her days meditating, or debating with and teaching the major religious figures of her era. During her lifetime, many sought out her company from afar in the hope of hearing her famous spiritually-inspired prose and reflections.

It is generally accepted that Al-ʿAdawiyya remained unmarried and childless throughout her life, although it has been reported that Ḥasan al-Baṣrī proposed marriage to her.

Rābiʿa Al-ʿAdawiyya died around 185/801, leaving behind a sound reputation as a significant thinker in the development of Islamic understanding.

Charles Upton: *Doorkeeper of the Heart: Versions of Rabiʿa*. Vermont: Threshold Books, 1988.

ʿAlī ibn Abī Ṭālib

ʿAlī ibn Abī Ṭālib was born thirty years after the birth of the Prophet Muḥammad (peace be upon him) in 600 CE, and belonged to the most prestigious family of Makka and the tribe of Quraysh: Banū Hāshim. His father, Abū Ṭālib, was the uncle of the Prophet, who took ʿAlī as a young child into his home and raised him as his son. Therefore, ʿAlī ibn Abī Ṭālib was amongst the first to witness the commencement of Prophethood at the tender age of ten.

ʿAlī did not hesitate to convert to the new religion and from the outset defended its creed and Messenger with passion and courage. During the difficult times in Makka he endured the insults and isolation inflicted on the Muslims, but persevered relentlessly in the new faith.

ʿAlī and the Prophet had already developed a strong and nurturing relationship, and in Madīna this culminated in the marriage of ʿAlī to Fāṭima al-Zahra, the beloved daughter of Muḥammad (peace be upon him) and Khadīja. Through this union, the progeny of the Prophet Muḥammad (peace be upon him) would continue.

While in Madīna he proved himself to be a brave and loyal defender of the new Muslim society, and during the Caliphate of Abū Bakr, ʿUmar ibn Khaṭṭāb and ʿUthmān he supported their leadership under increasingly challenging times. He also played an active role in ensuring stability and unity within the community.

After the tragic murder of ʿUthmān in 35 AH, ʿAlī ibn Abī Ṭālib suddenly found himself as the Caliph of a Muslim society with many fractures and instabilities. He set out to establish peace and security and sought to deal with the various break-ups of allegiance then occurring.

The continued internal struggle for leadership and power eventually led to the assassination of ʿAlī ibn Abī Ṭālib during the month of Ramaḍan in 40/661. He had ruled to the best of his abilities for four years and nine months and was sixty-three years old at the time of his death.

Syed Ruzee: *Sermons, Letters & Sayings of Hazrat Ali.* Translated from the Arabic by Syed Mohammed Askari Jafery. India: Seerat-i-Zahra Committee, 1965.

Abū ʿAmr

A 12th century notable and poet of Cordova, Andalusia. His father was a respected minister of the state and a poet in his own right.

Mālik Ibn Anas

Mālik ibn Anas was born in 93/715 in the city of Madīna. The period of the Companions of the Prophet (peace be upon him) had just come to an end and their students, known as the *tābiʿūn*, were at the forefront of Islamic learning. This made the city the spiritual and educational capital of the Muslim world.

Imām Mālik came from a prestigious Yemeni family that had migrated to Madīna and quickly established themselves as a respectable and hospitable family, committed to the nurturing and growth of Islamic knowledge. As a student Mālik ibn Anas gained a sound grounding in the Islamic sciences and proved to be a keen learner with a retentive memory and inquisitive mind. He studied under some of the most prominent early scholars of Islam, many of whom had been students of some of the greatest Companions and family members of the Prophet.

As a result, after the completion of his formal studies, Mālik quickly established himself as a sound jurist and scholar of *Ḥadīth*. When necessary he would fearlessly defend his legal opinions and bear the social or political consequences, resulting on one occasion in being flogged by the governor of Madīna.

Mālik's famous work *Al-Muwaṭṭa'* is ground-breaking and his greatest contribution to Islamic knowledge. Through it he codified

Madīnan jurisprudence and set a precedent for all future schools of law. The Mālikī School of law, based on his *Al-Muwaṭṭa'*, is still heavily practised today in parts of North and West Africa.

Imām Mālik ibn Anas died in 179/795 at the age of eighty-six in Madīna, and was buried there. He dedicated his life to the spreading of the Prophetic traditions and example and his work had and continues to have a great influence on the lives of Muslims globally.

Ibn ʿArabī

Muḥammad ibn ʿAlī ibn ʿArabī was born in Murcia, southern Spain in 560/1165. He came from a pious family with traditions in Sufism and this reflected in his early interest in matters of religion.

Ibn ʿArabī took advantage of culturally rich Muslim Spain, and received his initial education in the Qur'ān and principles of Islamic Law in Lisbon. He then spent the next thirty years travelling the region in pursuit of knowledge, also entering North Africa.

As a young man Ibn ʿArabī's reputation spread significantly. The famous jurist and philosopher Ibn Rushd (Averroes) is known to have requested his company.

In 1201 Ibn ʿArabī decided to make the pilgrimage to Makka at the age of thirty-five. He chose to stay on and teach in the Holy City, where he developed reputation as an enlightened teacher and thinker. He also travelled on to Egypt, Syria, Iraq, Jerusalem and Asia Minor. During his travels he would often receive gifts, but then distribute them to the poor.

The volume of Ibn ʿArabī's work is unknown but he has mentioned three hundred of his own works.

Eventually Ibn ʿArabī chose to settle in Damascus, where he spent the final seventeen years of his life. He continued to teach and write, and died on 16th November 638/1240 at the age of seventy-six.

The significance of Ibn ʿArabī's work cannot be underestimated. The Islamic philosophy he developed throughout his life has challenged many orthodox views. Today his work still comes under attack and was even banned in Egypt in the late 70s. However, his mystical philosophy of Unity cannot be disregarded or ignored and his legacy has significantly influenced and shaped discourses within the Muslim and non-Muslim world.

Ibn ʿArabī: *101 Diamonds from the Oral Tradition of the Glorious Messenger Mohammed*. Translated and interpreted by Lex Hixon and Fariha Al-Jerrahi. New York: Pir Press, 2002.

Ibn ʿArabī: *Journey to the Lord of Power*. Translated from the Arabic by Rabia Terri Harris. London: East-West Publications, 1981.

Ibn ʿArabī: *Stations of Desires*. Translated from the Arabic by Michael A. Sellis. Jerusalem: IBIS Editions 2000.

Ron Landou: *The Philosophy of Ibn Arabi*. George Allen & Unwin Ltd, 1959.

ʿĀ'isha bint Abī Bakr

The daughter of the prominent Companion Abū Bakr, ʿĀ'isha was born in 603 or 605 CE, and was eight years old at the time of the migration to Madīna. She married the Prophet (peace be upon him) at an early age in Makka, but did not live with him as his wife until a while after the migration to Madīna.

Due to her early and close contact with the Prophet, she was able to gain deep insight into the Qur'ān and witness the implementation of its teachings through his daily life. As a result ʿĀ'isha developed a keen intellect and sound knowledge of not only the Qur'ān but also various sciences such as Genealogy, History, Medicine and Literature.

From an early age she showed signs of an inquisitive mind and retentive memory. Consequently, many *Aḥādīth* clarifying theological and legalistic issues exist and have been preserved through her narration.

In married life the Messenger and ʿĀ'isha enjoyed a deep affection for each other. Their relationship was marked by consideration, respect and love. During his final illness the Prophet desired to spend his time at the home of ʿĀ'isha, and died while resting his head on her lap.

After the death of the Holy Prophet, ʿĀ'isha continued to play an active role in Muslim society. Her charitable acts and kind treatment of orphans were well known and her conduct remained noble and praiseworthy throughout her life. When the time was called for, ʿĀ'isha stood steadfast and strong in what she considered to be important issues for Muslim society and religion.

After the death of the fourth Caliph, ʿAlī ibn Abī Ṭālib, ʿĀ'isha withdrew into relative seclusion and lived out her final years in Madīna. She died there at the age of sixty-seven in 68/678. Her death caused great sadness across the Muslim land.

ʿĀ'isha's contribution to our understanding of how the Prophet (pbuh) conducted himself in his private life is so great, that without it Muslims would not fully appreciate the extent of his noble character and perfect example.

Rao Shamser Ali Khan and Fazl Ahmed: *Life of Aisha & Khadija.* International Islami Tabligh Mission.

Ṣalāḥ al-Dīn al-Ayyūbī

Ṣalāḥ al-Dīn al-Ayyūbī was born in 1137 in Damascus, into a chivalrous and military elite family; thus his early training and education was arranged to include a comprehensive subject area that tackled not only the religious and social studies of the time, but also the need for competent military warriors to fight the ongoing European Crusades into the Holy Land.

At the death of his uncle in 1169 CE Ṣalāḥ al-Dīn took on the position of Prime Minister of Egypt and proved himself a just and compassionate minister, leading to his taking the reigns of power at the death of the Caliph.

In 1174 CE the Crusaders laid siege to Damascus, and the deteriorating situation infuriated Ṣalāḥ al-Dīn so much that he returned to the city and in 1181-82 CE was acknowledged as the rightful ruler of the region.

During the early part of his reign Ṣalāḥ al-Dīn agreed a truce with the Franks in Palestine. However, this was broken and in 1187 CE he marched on the Franks and reoccupied a large number of cities, including Nablus, Jericho, Beirut and Asruf. He then turned his attention to Jerusalem, and despite sixty thousand Crusaders occupying the city, was able to recapture it in the same year.

The Crusaders had entered Jerusalem ninety years earlier, killing seventy thousand Muslims in the process. In 1187 CE Ṣalāḥ al-Dīn gave free pardon to the Christians living in the city and ordered combatants to leave on payment of a ransom. On leaving the Holy City many of the Christian refugees were refused entry into Christian strongholds by the rulers, and instead entered surrounding Muslim countries, where they were well-received and lived in relative security.

The fall of Jerusalem forced the Crusaders into action and Ṣalāḥ al-Dīn soon faced the combined military might of Europe. Crusader reinforcements flooded the region and Sulṭān Ṣalāḥ al-Dīn used his skill as a tactician and warrior to defend Muslim land. After severe fighting, peace was declared in the year 1192 CE and the Crusaders left the Holy Land, marking the end of the third Crusade.

During the months that followed Sulṭān Ṣalāḥ al-Dīn dedicated his time to social welfare, ensuring hospitals, schools and mosques were built throughout his domain. In 1193 CE he died in Damascus and the news of his passing sent the Muslim world into shock.

At his death it was found his worldly possessions amounted to his coat of mail, horse, one dinar and thirty-six dirhams.

Beha Ed-Din Abu El-Mehasan: *The Life of Saladin 1137-1193 AD.* New Delhi: Adam Publishers & Distributors, 1994.

Abū Bakr Al-Ṣiddīq

Abū Bakr is one of the most famous Companions of the Messenger (peace be upon him) and was born two years after him, in Makka. In his pre-Islamic days, he was a morally upright and abstinent man, well respected within Makkan society.

Among the first to accept Islam, Abū Bakr did not procrastinate in accepting the new faith. From the moment of his conversion he remained committed and steadfast in the face of the various repercussions Quraysh threw at the new community. During the difficult times in Makka, he encouraged the small community to be more public in their acts of worship, and spent much of his wealth to free converted slaves such as Bilāl.

His close friendship with the Prophet meant Abū Bakr was intimately involved in the development of the faith from the outset. He was fortunate enough to accompany the Prophet during his migration and was amongst the Ten People of the Garden (Companions guaranteed Paradise). He also became the Prophet's father-in-law, friend and confidant.

At the death of the Messenger (peace be upon him) the Muslim community went into shock and confusion spread. Abū Bakr was amongst those devastated, yet realising how Madīnan society was falling into crisis, he postponed his mourning and approached the people. Through his wise words he was able to restore calm and stability. He was appointed as first successor to the Prophet and set about establishing unity and justice. He worked hard to set the direction and future of Islam after the death of the Prophet (peace be upon him) towards a secure and fair society.

Abū Bakr died at the age of sixty-three from fever and illness. He ruled as *Khalīfa* for only two and a half years, yet his contribution and example to the Muslim community and the religion are still felt today.

Masadul Hasan: *Hazrat Abu-Bakr Siddique.* New Delhi: Kitab Bhavan.

Ḥasan Al-Baṣrī

Born during the reign of ʿUmar ibn al-Khaṭṭāb in the year 21 AH, Ḥasan al-Baṣrī was raised within the household of the Prophet Muḥammad's (peace be upon him) wife Umm Salamah. His father was a freed slave of Zayd ibn Thābit, a famous Companion of the Messenger of Allah.

From an early age, Ḥasan al-Baṣrī stood out for his intellectual depth and keenness to learn. The extent of his knowledge would only be fully understood by the world around him when, as an adult, he channelled it all into preserving the founding principles and values of the relatively new Muslim society.

As a young man Ḥasan al-Baṣrī was no doubt keen-witted enough to gauge the social and political changes taking place around him. He witnessed the growing trend towards materialism, the resurfacing of old tribal loyalties and various political struggles taking place within the Muslim community, and consequently he felt compelled to call people back to the guiding principles of spiritual richness and integrity.

As an adult, Ḥasan al-Baṣrī naturally moved into teaching, and was said to have the constant company of students that yearned to learn from him. Through his emotionally arousing and intellectually provoking preaching Ḥasan al-Baṣrī played a significant role in changing the social and spiritual direction of the Muslim society. His reputation grew greatly, and Ḥasan al-Baṣrī became an important member of his society, permeating its every fabric and influencing its direction and vision for the future.

He died in the year 110 AH at the age of eighty-nine in present day Syria, and his loss was felt throughout society. His funeral was held on a Friday and attended by the entire population of the city, resulting in the main mosque being deserted at the time of *ʿAṣr* prayer for the first time in its history.

Ibn Baṭṭūṭa

Abū ʿAbdullāh Muḥammad ibn Baṭṭūṭa was born in 703 AH/1304 AD in Tangiers, Morocco. Very little is known of his early life other than him receiving a comprehensive education and eventually studying law as a young man.

At the age of twenty-one, Ibn Bāṭṭūṭa left Tangiers to perform Ḥajj. Taking one and a half years to reach Makka, he passed through North Africa, Egypt, Palestine and Syria. On completion of the Ḥajj, Ibn Baṭṭūta visited Iraq and Persia in 1328 CE and from there moved on to modern day Tanzania, returning via Oman and the Persian Gulf to complete Ḥajj once more.

He then travelled through Syria and Egypt and headed for Asia Minor, crossing the Black Sea and entering West Central Asia. At this point he made a slight detour to Constantinople, but eventually headed in the direction of India, passing Afghanistan and arriving at the banks of the Indus River in 1333 CE.

Ibn Baṭṭūta spent eight years in India and took up the position of *Qāḍī* under the patronage of the Sulṭān of Delhi. Next he spent two more years travelling through Southern India, Ceylon and the Maldives Islands, and from there he made it to China, passing through Bengal, the coast of Borneo, Sumatra and Canton.

In 1346 to 1348 CE he returned to Makka to perform Ḥajj again, and then headed home to Morocco and arrived in Fez in 1349 CE. The temptation to travel overwhelmed him once more and Baṭṭūta visited Gibraltar and Granada in 1353 CE and also the Kingdom of Mali in West African Sudan. He returned to Morocco in 1355 CE.

It is estimated that Ibn Baṭṭūta travelled approximately 73,000 to 75,000 miles, further than Marco Polo and the furthest anyone had travelled before the invention of steam. In 1356 CE he was commissioned by the Sulṭān of Morocco, Abū ʿInān, to record his journeys in the form of a *Riḥla* (book of travels).

Ibn Baṭṭūta's *Riḥla* is not only a personal account of his experiences, but also a detailed record of 14th Century Muslim society, ranging from the most mundane aspects of daily human life to the most complex societal structures and practices. His contribution to geography and history is undeniable and the *Riḥla* is distinct in that it covers the breadth and width of Muslim land and culture.

Ibn Baṭṭūta made his final journey in 767/1368 and travelled on to his Lord at the age of sixty-four.

Ross E. Dunn: *The Adventures of Ibn Battuta, A Muslim Traveller of the 14th Century.* Kent: Croom Helm Ltd, 1986.

Ibn-Juzayy: *Ibn Battuta: Travels in Africa and Asia.* London: Routledge & Kegan Paul, 1929.

Al-Ghazālī

Abū Ḥāmid Muḥammad al-Ṭūsī al-Ghazālī was born in Ṭūs, in the province of Khurāsān, the north eastern region of present day Persia in 450/1058. As a child he went through the traditional education system.

In adulthood his reputation as a scholar and thinker grew and respect for his far-reaching knowledge expanded. Eventually he left Nīsābūr to join the courts of Niẓām al-Mulk, the powerful Seljuq Sulṭān's vizier. He left a lasting impression and his fame grew even further until he commanded respect amongst his peers.

At the young age of thirty-two Ghazālī was appointed principal of the Niẓāmiyya Madrasa, and the people of Baghdad were impressed by his lectures, eloquence and knowledge. Yet in 488/1094, he suddenly abandoned the wealth he had amassed, his fame and reputation and left in search of renunciation and solitude. He travelled to Makka where he completed Ḥajj and then moved on to Syria, Palestine and Egypt. During this period of his life Ghazālī spent much time in meditation, reflection and worship. In 492/1099 he returned to his hometown of Ṭūs, where he spent his time, compiling some of his most valuable books.

At the request of the vizier, Ghazālī returned to the Niẓāmiyya Madrasa to teach in 499/1106 and it was during this time in Baghdad that he wrote his famous *Iḥyā' 'Ulūm Al-Dīn* (Revival of Religious Sciences). He then began to use this work in delivering lectures at the school. Very soon after, he again withdrew from formal public life and returned to Ṭūs where he opened a *Madrasa* and *Khānqāh* (retreat).

Imām Al-Ghazālī passed away at the young age of fifty-three in the citadel of Ṭūs, and is rightfully credited with bringing Sufism to mainstream Muslim thought. Through his teaching and work he challenged the myths and stereotypes that surround the Sufi way.

Abū Ḥāmid Muhammad al-Ghazālī: *The Ninety-Nine Beautiful Names of God [Al-Maqṣad al-asnā Sharḥ asmā' Allāh al-ḥusnā]*. Translated from the Arabic by David B. Burrel & Nazih Daher. Cambridge: Islamic Texts Society, 1992.

Abū Ḥāmid Muḥammad al-Ghazālī: *The Book of Religious Learning, Vol III - Book of Worldly Usages [Iḥyā' 'Ulūm al-Dīn]*. Edited and translated from Arabic by Al-Haj Maulana Fazlul Karim. New Delhi: Islamic Book Service, 1991.

Abū Ḥāmid Muhammad al-Ghazālī: *The Book of Destructive Evils, Vol III – Book of Worldly Usages [Iḥyā' 'Ulūm al-Dīn]*. Edited and translated from the Arabic by Al-Haj Maulana Fazlul Karim. New Delhi: Islamic Book Service, 1982.

Abū Ḥāmid Muḥammad al-Ghazālī: *On Disciplining the Soul & Breaking the Two Desires [Iḥyā' 'Ulūm Al-Dīn]*. Translated from Arabic by T. J. Winter. Cambridge: Islamic Text Society, 1995.

Abū Ḥāmid Muḥammad al-Ghazālī: *The Remembrance of Death & the Afterlife [Iḥyā' 'Ulūm al-Dīn]*. Translated from Arabic by T. J. Winter. Cambridge: Islamic Text Society, 1989.

Abū Ḥāmid Muḥammad al-Ghazālī: *The Kings*. Translated from the Arabic by F.R.C. Bagley. London: Oxford University Press, 1964.

Ahmed Zidaan: *Revitalisation of the Sciences of Religion – Al-Ghazali's Ihya' Ulum al-Din*. Cairo: Islamic Inc. for Publishing and Distribution, 1997.

Al-Ḥaddād

Imām ʿAbdullāh ibn ʿAlawī al-Ḥaddād was born in the year 1044 AH in Tarīm, in the southern regions of the Arabian peninsula. He came from a prominent family that could trace its lineage back to the Prophet Muḥammad (peace be upon him) through Imām al-Ḥusayn.

Ḥaddād received classical education in the Islamic sciences that equipped him later in life for what he felt was a vital role of calling the masses to the Straight Path, in a time when people were going astray.

During his life Ḥaddād had a natural ability to detect the issues and conditions of his time and consequently understood the social and spiritual progress or stagnation of its people. He felt a responsibility to continue the legacy of his ancestors, and call people to a life filled with spiritual richness and social integrity. Consequently, he dedicated his life to teaching and writing, and in his work he deliberately chose to produce clear guidance, advice and instructions which were simple for the listeners or readers to understand and interpret into their own lives.

Imām al-Ḥaddād died in the year 1132 AH at the age of eighty-eight. He was buried in his hometown of Tarīm. The legacy he has left behind reflects the times within which he lived and wrote.

Imām ʿAbdullāh Ibn ʿAlawī Al-Ḥaddād: *Knowledge & Wisdom.* Translated from Arabic by Mostafa al-Badawi. Illinois: Starlatch Press, 2001.

Ḥāfiẓ

Khwāja Shams al-Dīn Muḥammad Ḥāfiẓ was born in Shīrāz in 1324 CE. Very little is known of his childhood and much of his life is shrouded in mystery and legend. However, most of the historians agree his poetry indicates a man with sound knowledge in both secular and religious sciences. His pen name 'Ḥāfiẓ' tells us that he memorised the whole of the Qur'ān, probably during his early childhood.

In his youth Ḥāfiẓ enjoyed the company of friends and indulged in various social activities. However, he soon gave it all up, choosing instead to dedicate his time and energy to spiritual development and poetry.

The only indication of Ḥāfiẓ ever marrying or fathering children is in his own writing, where he mourns the death of his beloved wife and sons.

In his poetry Ḥāfiẓ shows distaste for injustice and tyranny. He refused to bow to the pressures of religious zealots who sought to oppress in the name of religion and instead openly criticised their conduct in his writing. Ḥāfiz also wrote of matters of the heart, and his beautiful prose has continued to touch people from all cultures to this day. His style is considered unique within the literary world, challenging the sharpest of minds and pushing the reader to greater levels of self-awareness. His '*Dīwān*' is a fine example of the literary heights Persian poetry has reached in Muslim history and indicates a man of immense spiritual depth.

Ḥāfiẓ seemed to have no great desire to preserve his work and on his death in 1391 CE his poetry was unorganised and scattered. However, through the diligent work of a close companion it was authenticated and gathered into one volume.

Shams-Ud-Din Muhammed Hafiz-I-Shirazi: *The Divan-i-Hafiz – VOL II & I.* Translated from Arabic by Liet-Col. H. Wilbertorcc Clarke. New York: Samuel Weiser Inc, 1989.

Aḥmad ibn Muḥammad ibn Ḥanbal

Abū ʿAbdullāh Aḥmad ibn Muḥammad ibn Ḥanbal was born in Marw in 164 AH. His father was a famous scholar who died at a young age and his mother moved to Baghdad, where she took on the responsibility of raising him and ensuring that he gained adequate education.

As a young student Imām Ibn Ḥanbal showed himself to have an inquisitive mind and retentive memory. He pursued classical education and at the age of sixteen began to specialise in *Ḥadīth*. As a young man he travelled to the Arabian peninsula extensively in search of *Aḥādīth*, studying under many scholars of repute including Imām Shāfiʿī.

He chose to live a very ascetic life, only ever possessing what was enough for physical survival. He refused to accept people's *Ṣadaqa* and instead would offer some service in exchange for provisions. He also shied away from positions of authority and government circles, although he was a well-known and respected scholar.

In his later years Imām Ibn Ḥanbal came into conflict with various rulers and was eventually taken to prison in chains, where he was put into solitary confinement and severely tortured. Despite this he continued to deny the legitimacy of certain ideas prevalent amongst government circles, and stood by his condemnation of innovated ideology.

Imām Ibn Ḥanbal's famous work, *Al-Musnad*, and other writings have formed the basis for one of the four schools of Sunnī thought still adhered to today.

The Imām died in 241 AH at the age of seventy-seven. At the time of his death Ibn Ḥanbal had gained mass respect and it has been reported that hundreds of thousands of people followed his funeral cortège through the streets of Baghdad.

Ibn Ḥazm

ʿAlī Ibn Aḥmad Ibn Saʿīd Ibn Ḥazm al-Andalusī was born in 384/994 in Andalus, Spain. He was born into a privileged home and raised in an aristocratic way. As a child he studied Arabic, poetry, the Qur'ān, calligraphy and Latin.

In adulthood Ibn Ḥazm played an active role in his society and was involved in scholarly and political activities. He held the post of minister on three separate occasions but was also thrown into prison three times.

Ibn Ḥazm married and fathered three children. He personally took on the responsibility of their education and taught them a range of Islamic and classical sciences.

Despite the criticism Ibn Ḥazm faced for his literary work during his life, he was, and still is considered an authoritative figure on *fiqh*, and his contributions to philosophical debates in Islam are still relevant today. His work on morality forms a basis for social and individual development that shows a deep insight into the human condition.

Ibn Ḥazm lived a volatile life, often offending his peers and the government, yet he stood firmly by his political and philosophical beliefs and bore the consequences. He pushed the debates of his time to further limits that ultimately threw up new ideas and exposed old ones to greater scrutiny. He died at the age of seventy, in 456 AH/1056 CE.

Ibn Hazm al-Andalusi: *In Pursuit of Virtue.* London: Taha Publishers, 1990.

Ibn ʿAṭā' Allāh al-Iskandarī

Tāj al-Dīn Abū'l-Faḍl Aḥmad ibn Muḥammad ibn ʿAbd al-Karīm ibn ʿAṭā' Allāh al-Iskandarī al-Judhamī al-Shādhilī was born in Alexandria, Egypt around the mid seventh/thirteenth century. He came from a respected family of Mālikī jurists and his grandfather was a renowned writer on jurisprudence and Arabic language.

In his youth al-Iskandarī was educated within the traditional fields of Islamic sciences and studied under some of the most prominent scholars of Alexandria. With the guidance of both his father and grandfather his education was thorough, covering Qur'ānic Recitation, Prophetic Traditions, Arabic and Grammar, Philosophy, Principles of Jurisprudence and Law.

By his mid-twenties al-Iskindarī had already developed a reputation as a competent Mālikī scholar. At first, like his grandfather he was sceptical and hostile to Sufism and the Sufi community of Egypt. However, this changed virtually overnight when he met Shaykh Abū'l-ʿAbbās al-Mursī. While continuing his work as a Mālikī scholar, al-Iskandarī spent the next twelve years as a devout disciple of al-Mursī.

During this time al-Iskandarī's reputation as a Mālikī scholar grew and he became an authority in Islamic *Sharīʿa* law and Islamic Mysticism. Through his scholarship, in-depth knowledge, love and commitment to both areas he was able to develop an Islamic worldview that gave importance to and balanced both the inner and outer forms of worship and Muslim life.

During the later part of his life al-Iskandarī took part in a public debate with ibn Taymiyya to refute his criticisms of ibn ʿArabī. The event attracted the attention of many and was attended by hundreds of students and laymen alike.

Ibn ʿAṭā' Allāh al-Iskandarī died two years after the debate in the year 709/1309 at around sixty years of age. His efforts to merge the outer and inner forms of Muslim worship and life have been compared to Imām Ghazālī, and his contribution to the debate concerning the role of Sufism in orthodox religion is significant.

Ibn ʿAṭāʾ Allāh al-Iskandarī: *The Key to Salvation: A Sufi Manual.* Cambridge: Islamic Texts Society, 1996.

Jaʿfar Ibn ʿAbī Ṭālib

Before the advent of Islam Muḥammad (peace be upon him) was already known as an honest and righteous individual. As he witnessed his uncle Abū Ṭālib struggle in poverty with heavy family responsibilities, he felt compelled to ease the burden. Therefore he approached his other uncle, al-ʿAbbās, and both agreed they should each take one of Abū Ṭālib's sons and raise them as their own. Muḥammad took ʿAlī ibn Abī Ṭālib and Jaʿfar ibn Abī Ṭālib was raised in the household of al-ʿAbbās.

As a young man Jaʿfar married and established a home for himself and his new wife in Makka. At the commencement of Prophethood they were amongst the first households of Makka to accept Islam. This immediately exposed them to the rage of Quraysh and they, along with the other new Muslims, were subject to continuous public humiliation and persecution. Jaʿfar and his wife bore the physical injury and social and economic isolation with patience and steadfastness.

Jaʿfar yearned to practise and nurture his new faith in a safe environment and so eventually migrated to the land of Abyssinia (present day Ethiopia) with his family and a small band of Companions.

When Quraysh learned of the migrant's state of freedom and security in Abyssinia, they set out to have the group extradited back to Makka. Their attempts to bribe the bishops of the royal court with gifts and convince the Negus of the treason of the Muslim group failed because of Jaʿfar ibn Abī Ṭālib's eloquent description of Islam and its purpose, when called to explain the new religion.

The Muslims lived under the protection of the Negus for ten years and Jaʿfar's wife gave birth to three children, naming one Muḥammad after the Holy Prophet and setting a trend that has lasted to this day.

Eventually, in the seventh year after Hijra and again under the leadership of Jaʿfar ibn Abī Ṭālib they set off to join their fellow companions in Madīna. Instantly Ja'far became concerned for the welfare of the poor of Madīna and would distribute his own food to ease their suffering.

In the eighth year after Hijra, Ja'far set out with an army to face Byzantine forces. After putting up a brave and fearless fight he fell on the battlefield while commanding the Muslim army.

Al-Jāḥiẓ

Abū 'Uthmān 'Amr ibn Baḥr al-Kinānī al-Fuqaymī al-Baṣrī, otherwise known as al-Jāḥiẓ because of his protruding eye, was born in Baṣra, the principal city of southern Iraq in 160/776. Very little is known of his lineage except that he was of African descent and that his ancestors had been slaves.

There is little information about his early childhood and youth, other than that it was spent in his native city of Baṣra, where he attended the Qur'ān school within Banū Fuqaym district. Due to his social position, his education was, in all likelihood, limited and incomplete. Therefore, the knowledge he acquired was through sheer determination and a love of study.

Initially al-Jāḥiẓ simply wandered the city of Baṣra picking up an understanding of Arabic language, poetry and culture. He would join the gathered students of prominent scholars with no particular attachment to the school. This lifestyle exposed him to some of the great teachers and thinkers of his time, and eventually al-Jāḥiẓ developed a sound and thorough knowledge of poetry, grammar, logic and various other sciences.

With such an informal education, the direction al-Jāḥiẓ took in his studies and later writing was very much influenced by the issues and concerns of his time and region. His published Mu'tazilite treatise on the caliphate soon won him the favour of the ruler al-Ma'mūn, and his life as a poor independent student began to reap its rewards, as his reputation as an important thinker and commentator of his time grew.

With the support of al-Ma'mūn, al-Jāḥiẓ moved to Baghdad and lived there for almost fifty years, surviving through bouts of teaching and other work. Again the thirst for knowledge affected him and al-Jāḥiẓ took advantage of Baghdad and its reputation as the centre of learning. He attended various mosques, study circles and classes of scholars around the city and consolidated his existing knowledge.

Because of al-Jāḥiẓ's independence as a student and lack of attachment to a particular school or teacher, his skills as a thinker were further sharpened. uninhibited by a set programme of study. Consequently, his writing style and content proved and still does prove to be unique.

Eventually, al-Jāḥiẓ retired to his hometown of Baṣra around 247/861 brought about by old age, failing health and political changes within Baghdad. He spent his last years in Baṣra writing in his library, and it is not surprising that in his early to mid-nineties he died there, surrounded by his most treasured possessions, his books, in 255/868.

Al-Jāḥiẓ: *The Book of Misers.* Translated from Arabic by Prof. R. B. Sergeant. Reading: The Centre for Muslim Contribution to Civilisation, 1997.

Charles Pellat: *The Life & Works of Jāḥiẓ – Translation of Selected Texts.* Translated from the French by D. M. Hawke. London: Routledge & Kegan Paul, 1969.

Ibn al-Jawzī

Born in 508 AH in Baghdad, Ibn al-Jawzī was raised during an intellectually rich period of Muslim history and within the walls of a famously progressive city of the Islamic world.

His father died while Ibn al-Jawzī was still a young child and his mother took on the responsibility of ensuring that he had a thorough education. From a young age he showed an intense yearning for knowledge, and would spend his days attending lectures and reading in the numerous Baghdad libraries, while his peers would watch street entertainers around the city centre. He had a particular zeal for authenticating, collecting and memorising traditions of the Prophet Muḥammad (pbuh) and soon developed a reputation as an authority on the sciences of *Ḥadīth*. He began writing at an early age and continued throughout his life.

As a young man Ibn al-Jawzī continued in his pursuit of knowledge and was known for his piety and religious devotion. As in his childhood, he avoided the entertainment that the vibrant city of Baghdad offered and chose instead to spend his evenings in prayer and recitation of the Holy Qur'ān. His lectures were in high demand within the city and attracted a range of listeners from far and wide, including caliphs, governors and officials of the state. In fact, the estimated number of regular attendees of his lectures ranges from ten to fifteen thousand.

He died in 587 AH in Baghdad at the age of seventy-nine, and it has been reported that the whole of Baghdad came to a standstill for his funeral procession.

Ibn Qayyim al-Jawziyya

Shams al-Dīn Muḥammad ibn Abī Bakr ibn Qayyim al-Jawziyya was born in 691/1292 in al-Zurʿa, a small farming village fifty-five miles outside of Damascus. Very little is known of his childhood except that his father was the principal of the famous Hanablite school, al-Jawziyya. However, we do know that al-Jawziyya received a comprehensive Islamic education, specialising in Ḥanbalī *Fiqh*.

As a young student he came under the influence of Muʿtazilite teachings until 712/1312 when, at the age of twenty-one, Ibn Qayyim met Ibn Taymiyya. Their friendship was to last sixteen years and shaped al-Jawziyya's growth and orientation in Islam. In fact it was only the death of ibn Taymiyya that separated the two friends.

Between 712/1312 and 726/1326 Ibn Qayyim taught at his father's school. However, nearing the end of 726/1326 the authorities in Damascus ordered the arrest of Ibn Taymiyya and his loyal followers. Ibn Qayyim al-Jawziyya was amongst those imprisoned, and when Ibn Taymiyya's followers were released a few days later, he chose to remain with his friend and teacher in prison.

In 728/1328 Ibn Taymiyya died in prison, and it was only then that Jawziyya chose to leave his voluntary confinement and join the funeral procession. He spent the rest of his life writing, teaching and travelling. His famous student, Ibn Kathīr, preserved the last twenty-five years of Jawziyya's life's work and became, in his own right, a respected commentator of the Qur'ān.

Ibn Qayyim al-Jawziyya died in 751/1350 at the age of sixty. His funeral was held in the Umayyad Mosque, Damascus and he was buried near his father by Bāb al-Ṣaghīr.

Ibn-Qayyim Al-Jawziyya: *The Invocation of God.* London: Islamic Texts Society, 2000.

Ibn Qayyim Al-Jawziyya: *Implements for the Patient, Supplies for the Grateful – The Way to Patience & Gratitude.* Edited and Translated from Arabic by Chanicka & Salma Cook. Al-Mansura: Umm al-Qura Publishers, 2000.

Ibn Qayyim Al-Jawziyya: *Medicine of the Prophet.* Translated from Arabic by Penelope Johnstone. Cambridge: Islamic Text Society, 1998.

Al-Jīlānī

Shaykh ʿAbd al-Qādir al-Jīlānī was born in Gīlān, in the western region of modern day Iran in 470/1077. His lineage can be traced back to the Prophet Muḥammad (peace be upon him) through both his father and mother. At the death of his father Jīlānī continued to live with his mother until the age of eighteen, at which point he moved to Baghdad.

In Baghdad he attached himself as a student to two well-known scholars: Abū Saʿīd ʿAlī al-Mukharrimī and then Abū'l-Khayr Ḥammād al-Dabbās. He then chose to leave Baghdad and spent the next twenty-five years wandering the deserts and ruins of Iraq as a hermit, experiencing solitude and reflection.

Eventually in 521/1127 Jīlānī returned to the city at over fifty years of age. He began to lecture at the school of his old teacher al-Makharrimī and his reputation as a profound thinker and eloquent speaker grew at a staggering speed. He spoke of the concerns of his time and managed to affect the hearts and minds of those around him, often attracting hundreds of students. The school proved too small to accommodate the demand for his circles and eventually an extension with living quarters was built.

Jīlānī would often leave his work to attend to the needs of the poor, slaves, and children and would assist them with general household chores, such as washing clothes.

There are numerous works of Jīlānī's still available today and the recent translation of his work into English has given him a new audience of Muslims and non-Muslims and resulted in a revival of his thinking.

ʿAbd al-Qādir al-Jīlānī died in Baghdad at the age of ninety, in the year 561/1166. He died in the presence of his sons, who were able to preserve his last inspiring words.

Shaykh ʿAbd al-Qādir al-Jīlānī: *Jilā' Al-Khāṭir [Purification of the Mind]*. Edited by Sheikh Muhammad Al-Casazani Al-Husseini and translated from Arabic by Prof. Shetha Al-Dargazelli & Louay Fatoohi. Kuala Lumpar: A. S. Noordeen, 1999.

Muhtar Holland: *Utterances of Sheikh Abdal Qadir al-Jilani*. Fort Lauderdale: Al-Baz Publishing Inc, 1988.

Sheikh Abdal-Qadir al-Jilani: *The Removal of Cares [Jalā' al-Khawāṭir – A collection of Forty-Five Discourses]*. Translated from Arabic by Muhtar Holland. Fort Lauderdale: Al-Baz Publishing Inc, 1997.

Al-Junayd

Abū'l-Qāsim al-Junayd ibn Muḥammad ibn al-Junayd Khazzāz al-Qawārīr was born around 215 AH/818 CE in Baghdad. Little is known of his childhood except that his paternal uncle, Sarī al-Saqaṭī, raised him in Baghdad after the death of his father, while still a young child. He came from a family of merchants and as an adult continued in the family tradition, choosing to specialise in the trading of raw silk.

At the age of thirty Junayd turned to Sufism and spent the next ten years studying under some of the most influential scholars in Baghdad.

As a student and later teacher at his uncle's school, Junayd would only sit in small private study circles and, like his uncle, continued to conceal the doctrine of the school to the public at large, for fear of being misunderstood. Later in life, Junayd felt the masses had become more exposed to the Sufi way and thus became more confident in preaching to wider audiences, although he remained hesitant to preach publicly.

His successful trade in raw silk left him considerably wealthy; however, Junayd chose to live a very modest lifestyle and used his wealth to help the poor, opening his house to struggling students.

In his later life Sufism came under attack within Baghdad and Junayd was accused of heresy. His lifelong fear of his particular doctrine becoming misinterpreted and misunderstood by the public and various government institutions turned into reality and Junayd, along with other teachers of the school, faced charges of apostasy.

Eventually the school was cleared of the charges and allowed to continue in its work, but Junayd became increasingly private and resentful of the effects of the trial.

He lived until an old age, spending his last years in relative seclusion and died in 296/908.

Although al-Junayd did not enjoy mass popularity across the Muslim world during his lifetime, the writing he has left behind has had an important influence on how Sufism has evolved.

Abdul Kadir Ali Hassan: *The Life, Personality and Writings of Al-Junayd*. London: Luzac & Company Ltd, 1962.

Al-Jurjānī

His full name was Abū'l-Ḥasan ʿAbd al-ʿAzīz al-Jurjānī. He was an 11th century Arab philologist who died in 1078 CE.

Ibn Kathīr

Abū'l-Fidā Ismāʿīl ibn Abī Ḥafṣ Shihāb al-Dīn ʿUmar ibn Kathīr was born in the town of Buṣra, Syria in the year 701 AH. His father was a respected member of his community and would deliver the *Khuṭba* (sermon) at Friday prayers. However, Ibn Kathīr was orphaned at four years old, leaving him to be raised by his brother.

In 706 AH the family moved to Damascus and the young Ibn Kathīr began his studies. He underwent a comprehensive education, providing him with a thorough knowledge of all the main sciences and fields of study deemed important in his time. He excelled in learning, impressing both his teachers and fellow students, and was particularly well known for his accurate and vast retention of Prophetic traditions and his sharp mind in jurisprudence.

Eventually Ibn Kathīr used the knowledge he acquired to issue religious edicts for the community within which he lived. He was also a prolific writer and made a massive contribution to the Muslim literary world. His famous commentary of the Holy Qur'ān is widely available today in many languages and still read as a source of further understanding of the Qur'ān's message. His biography of the Prophet Muḥammad (pbuh) is considered an essential historical account of the events and circumstances surrounding the Prophet's life and that of the early Muslims.

Ibn Kathīr died in 774 AH in Damascus at the age of seventy-three.

Ibn Kathīr: *Tafsir Al-Qur'ān.* London: Al-Firdous Ltd, 1996.

Ibn Khaldūn

Ibn Khaldūn's forefathers migrated to Seville in the 9th century CE and for almost four centuries Seville's rulers employed various members of the family as administrators and statesmen. By the 13th century they were a ruling family of Seville.

Consequent upon the Christian occupation, like many notables, the family chose to go into exile in Tunis and ʿAbd al-Raḥmān Walī al-Dīn Muḥammad Ibn Khaldūn was born in there in 732/1332. As a child he studied traditional education, including the Qur'ān, Qur'ānic Sciences, Arabic, *Ḥadīth* and Jurisprudence.

In 1354 CE the ruler Abū ʿInān invited Ibn Khaldūn to complete his studies in Fez, Morocco. On completing his education he married and took up a clerical position in Abū ʿInān's administration, but at some point he fell out with the ruler and was imprisoned for a short time. At the death of Abū ʿInān in 1358 CE, Ibn Khaldūn was released from prison and became involved in politics. In 1359 CE he was made Secretary of State and continued in that position until 1361 CE.

Due to political instability within North Africa, Ibn Khaldūn decided to leave Fez and arrived in Granada in 1362 CE. The next eight years were his most tumultuous politically, and a second imprisonment left him feeling disillusioned. He began to feel a desire to withdraw from public life and return to scholarly research, and in 1378 CE was able to fulfil his ambition and return to Tunis. There he spent his time teaching and began writing his influential book *History*.

In 1384 CE Ibn Khaldūn migrated to Cairo, Egypt. His wife and children were due to join him soon after, but their ship sank and all were drowned. Ibn Khaldūn was devastated by his loss, but chose to stay on in Egypt. At this stage he had completed *History,* and became a Qāḍī (judge) and president of the well-known Al-Azhar University. Ibn Khaldūn threw himself into his teaching and research, becoming a professor of Mālikī jurisprudence and eventually Chief Mālikī Judge of Egypt.

Ibn Khaldūn died unexpectedly at the age of seventy-four in 806/1406. He is buried in the Sufi cemetery outside Cairo's Naṣr Gate.

The contribution his *History* has made to the academic world is immense. In recent years many academics have begun to acknowledge Ibn Khaldūn's rightful place as the forefather of Social Sciences. *The Muqaddima (Introduction to History)* arguably contains the foundations upon which modern-day Sociology is built.

Ibn Khaldūn: *The Muqaddimah (An Introduction to History) – 3 Vols.* Translated from Arabic by Franz Rosenthal. New York: Bollingen Foundation Inc, 1958.

Heinrich Simion: *Ibn Khaldun's Science of Human Culture.* Translated by Fuad Baali. Lahore: Ashraf Printing Press, 1978.

ʿUmar ibn al-Khaṭṭāb

ʿUmar ibn al-Khaṭṭāb was amongst the righteous Companions of the Prophet (peace be upon him), and one of the Ten People of the Garden (guaranteed Paradise).

Before the advent of Islam he was amongst the Makkan nobility and had considerable influence within its various tribes. He had been amongst those who persecuted the new Muslim community and showed great hatred to their message.

However, ʿUmar ibn al-Khaṭṭāb accepted Islam at the age of twenty-six in the sixth year of prophecy, and as a new Muslim threw all his influence, energy and wealth into the spreading of the new religion and the defence of its followers. Instead of worshipping in private from fear of retribution, ibn al-Khaṭṭāb publicly declared his belief in Islam and practised its rituals openly within the hostile Makkan society.

His conversion strengthened Islam, as the Prophet had prayed it would, and gave the small but growing Muslim community confidence in themselves and their future.

ʿUmar ibn al-Khaṭṭāb became not only a champion of the new religion but also a close and dear friend of the Prophet Muḥammad (peace be upon him). The number of *Aḥādīth* transmitted through him is testament to the amount of time spent in the Prophet's company and the diverse nature and rich quality of their conversations.

ʿUmar ibn al-Khaṭṭāb also experienced and actively took part in all of the victories and struggles of the first Muslims.

On the death of Abū Bakr, ʿUmar ibn al-Khaṭṭāb was elected leader of the Muslims in 13 AH. During his leadership Damascus, modern day Jordan and Jerusalem were conquered, and he also extended the Prophet's Mosque in Madīna in 17 AH.

On returning from the Ḥajj, ʿUmar was killed while leading the prayer. The loss was greatly felt throughout the Muslim world, and his leadership based on justice and humanity has set a fine example for mankind.

Shibli Numani: *Al-Farooq. The Life of Omar the Great: Second Caliph of Islam.* Translated from Urdu by Maulana Zafar Ali Khan. New Delhi: International Islamic Publishers, 1992.

Abū Madyan

Abū Madyan Shuʿayb ibn al-Ḥusayn al-Anṣārī was born in 509/1115-1116 in Seville, a region of Muslim Spain.

Abū Madyan was orphaned at an early age and his elder brothers took on the responsibility of his upbringing. However, as a child he was mistreated and deprived of a comprehensive education. He eventually fled in search of Islamic knowledge and found himself in the port of Sebta and then Marrakesh, the capital of the Almoravid state. In Marrakesh he was drafted into the military and again mistreated by his peers.

His search for knowledge took him to the famous Qarawiyyīn mosque and university in Fez and there he learnt to perform ablution and pray, and began to attend regular study circles.

He moved on to the middle Atlas region in order to study at the feet of the famous Sufi Shaykh Al-Dukkālī. From there he travelled to Bijāya where he began to develop reputation as a great teacher and spiritual guide, until he became famous throughout the Maghrib. Over a thousand respected spiritual leaders in Western Africa are known to have been his students.

Abū Madyan remained celibate most of his life except for a black concubine that he kept for a short time.

At the age of 85 he was called back to the capital to answer allegations regarding his activities in Bijāya by the authorities. He never made it, and died of illness and old age during the journey. His last words are reported to have been: "God is the Truth."

Vincent J Cornell: *The Way of Abū Madyan – The Works of Abū Madyan.* Cambridge: Islamic Texts Society, 1996.

Al-Mahdī

12th century ruler of present day Morocco, based in Marrakesh. Died in 1130 CE.

Al-Muqaddisī

His full name was Shaykh ʿIzz al-Dīn ibn ʿAbd al-Salām ibn Aḥmad ibn Ghānim al-Muqaddisī and he was a prominent Sufi thinker of the thirteenth century CE. He died in the year 1280 CE.

His famous work *The Revelation of the Secrets of the Birds and Flowers* was inspired by a day spent in a large garden, absorbing and contemplating the natural world around him.

Al-Muqaddisi: *The Revelation of the Secrets of the Birds and Flowers.* Translated from Arabic by Irene Hoare & Darya Galy. London: Octagon Press, 1979.

Al-Nawawī

Muḥyī al-Dīn Abū Zakariyā Yaḥyā ibn Sharaf al-Nawawī was born in the village of Nawā, south of Damascus, Syria in 631/1233.

At the age of eighteen he travelled with his father to Damascus to continue his studies. He excelled in Shāfiʿī *fiqh* and his zeal for learning continued unabated. He would often attend up to twelve lectures a day on different subjects, and overall his lifestyle was organised around learning. At the age of twenty-four Nawawī began teaching at the famous Ashrafiyya School. His reputation as an insightful teacher with far-reaching knowledge grew and spread across the region.

His famous work includes his *Forty Ḥadīth* and *Riyāḍ al-Ṣāliḥīn* (Gardens of the Righteous), both available today in English.

Nawawī eventually returned to his hometown of Nawā and died shortly after at the young age of forty-four in 676/1277.

Al-Nawawi: *Commentary on the Forty Hadith*. Translated from Arabic by Jamaal Al-Din & M. Zarabozo. Boulder: Al-Basheer, 1999.

Imām Abū Zakariyā Yaḥyā ibn Sharaf An-Nawawī: *Riyadh us-Saliheen*. Karachi: International Islamic Publishers, 1986.

Al-Qushayrī

Abū'l-Qāsim ibn Hawāzin ibn ʿAbd al-Malik ibn Ṭalḥa al-Qushayrī was born in 376 /986 in a town near the city of Nishapur, Khurāsān. As a child he received a thorough education in the traditional sciences and memorised the Qur'ān.

As a young student Qushayrī moved to Nishapur to study Mathematics and hoped to eventually work for the Ghaznavid administration. However, Nishapur was increasingly becoming the centre of Islamic intellectual and scholarly growth, and soon Qushayrī changed his plans and attached himself to the prominent Sufi teacher Shaykh al-Daqqāq, as a novice.

Both student and teacher soon developed a special bond, and while Qushayrī was sent to different theologians to study the various sciences Shaykh al-Daqqāq personally oversaw his inner spiritual growth and education.

While in his fifties the city of Nishapur was captured by the Seljuks and Qushayrī soon came into conflict with the new government. In an attempt to spread their preferred school of thought the Seljuks set about suppressing some Islamic opinions and encouraging the circulation of others. Al-Qushayrī was amongst those who publicly challenged the rulers and their actions and soon he was arrested and imprisoned within the citadel of Nishapur. He was rescued from prison by a band of his followers and fled, making his way to the safe haven of Makka.

Along with four hundred other judges and scholars, Qushayrī remained exiled from his land and lived under the constant threat of persecution until the death of the Seljuk leader Toghril Bey, at which point he returned to Nishapur and lived in relative peace for a further eight years.

Al-Qushayrī died in the year 465/1072 in Nishapur, where he was buried alongside his father-in-law and teacher, al-Daqqāq.

Abū al-Qāsim al-Qushayrī: *Sufi Book of Spiritual Ascent [Al-Risāla Al-Qushayriyya]*. Translated from Arabic by Rabia Harris. Chicago: Kazi Publications Inc, 1997.

Sayyid Quṭb

Sayyid Quṭb Ibrāhīm Ḥusayn al-Shādhilī was born in 1906 in the small village of Musha in northern Egypt.

On completing his education Sayyid Quṭb worked as a teacher for six years and as a school inspector for the Ministry of Education during the 1930s and 1940s. With the end of World War II, social and economic injustices, political corruption and continuing Western ideological influence all emerged as factors inhibiting Egypt's progress. This radically changed Quṭb's ideological orientation, leading to the publication of his first book *Social Justice in Islam*.

At the age of forty-two, Sayyid Quṭb travelled to America to study its education system with already strong views about Western lifestyles. His experiences in America only confirmed his existing views that Western culture was devoid of spiritual content and driven by materialism.

In 1952 he returned to Egypt a different man and joined the Muslim Brotherhood. During this time he engaged in what he felt was a revolutionary and necessary push to transform Muslim society into one based socially, economically and legally on the principles and laws laid out in the Qur'ān. In the same year he published the first volume of the twenty-nine-volume *tafsir* 'In the Shade of the Qur'ān', and in 1954 was arrested along with other Muslim Brotherhood members.

Sayyid Quṭb spent most of the rest of his life in prison, where he suffered severe torture, punishment and humiliation. In 1957, President Nasser got killed twenty Muslim Brotherhood members and Qutb's work became more radical as a result.

In 1964 he was released from prison at the request of the Iraqi president and it was during this short-lived freedom that he wrote his work *Milestones*. He was rearrested in 1966 and jailed for conspiring against the Egyptian government. On August 21 1966 Sayyid Quṭb was hanged.

Sayyid Quṭb: *In the Shade of the Qur'ān*. London: MWH Publishers, 1979. 12 volumes of this *tafsīr* under the same title have been so far published by the Islamic Foundation, Leicester

Sayyid Qutb: *Milestones*. The Holy Koran Publishing House, 1978.

Fakhr al-Dīn al-Rāzī

Abū ʿAbdullāh Abū al-Faḍl Muḥammad ibn ʿUmar al-Rāzī was born at Rayy, in present-day Iran, during the month of Ramaḍān in 543 or 544/1149 or 1150. He was born into a prominent Shāfiʿite and Ashʿarite family and educated as a young child by his father.

As a young student he developed a thorough knowledge of the Islamic Sciences and travelled to other parts of the Persian world, suffering ill health and tribulations along the way. Eventually, he returned to Rayy, where he quickly developed a reputation as a profound thinker and charismatic orator.

Ibn Taymiyya later criticised the Imām, arguing that through one of his works al-Rāzī promoted star-worship and sorcery. However, again there is little evidence of this and instead it seemed to focus on the hidden mysteries of astrology. Other scholars have claimed Imām al-Rāzī did not even write the book concerned.

Later in life the effects of bearing and answering to the various allegations took their toll and Imām al-Rāzī became disillusioned by the world around him.

Regardless of the various accusations levied against al-Rāzī and their truth or falsehood, his contribution to Islamic philosophy is undisputed. He died in the year 606/1209 at around the age of sixty, after a continued turbulent and controversial last few years.

Abū Bakr Muḥammad ibn Zakariyā al-Rāzī: *ʿIlm al-Akhlāq: The Book of Soul and Spirit and an Exposition of their Faculties*. Translated from the Arabic by M. Saghir Hassan Maʿsumi. Islamabad: Islamic Research Institute, 1969.

Jalāl al-Dīn Rūmī

Mawlānā Jalāl al-Dīn Rūmī was born in 604/1207 in Balkh, in the province of Khurāsān, the northwest region of present day Iran. He was a descendent of Abū Bakr al-Ṣiddīq on his father's side and came from a highly respected family of scholars and jurists. While still a child, Rūmī's father had to flee Balkh and chose to take the young boy with him. They travelled for sixteen years, eventually settling in Konya, at which point Rūmī was in his early twenties.

After the death of his father, Rūmī continued his education, eventually travelling to Aleppo and Damascus, Syria, to study at their prominent universities. He then returned to Konya where he began writing and teaching. Soon his fame as a deep thinker and teacher grew, and students attended his classes in droves.

During this time he came into contact with Shams Tabrīz. The latter had a profound effect on Rūmī, culminating in him becoming his spiritual mentor and guide. The bond between the two grew to great heights and Rūmī relied heavily on Shams Tabrīz's advice and guidance. This consequently caused resentment among Rūmī's disciples.

He spent the rest of his time in meditation and writing and died in the year 672/1273 at the age of sixty-eight in Konya. His funeral attracted thousands of Muslims, and many Jews and Christians also joined the mourners.

Rūmī was amongst the first Sufis to introduce the notion of dance and music as part of worship. The famous Whirling Dervishes are descendants of his branch of Sufism and incorporate symbolic dance into spiritual growth and progression.

His famous book *The Mathnawī* is amongst the most inspiring of Sufi literature and has had a profound impact on human spiritual health. Taking over forty years to complete, *The Mathnawī* pushes the soul to reach its spiritual potential.

Reynold A. Nicholson: *The Mathnawi of Jalalud-din Rumi*. New Delhi: Adam Publishers & Distributors, 1930.

Ibn Rushd

Abū'l-Walīd Muḥammad ibn Aḥmad ibn Muḥammad ibn Rushd, also known by his Latin name Averroes, was born in 520/1125 in Cordova.

He received a high standard in traditional education, studying *Fiqh*, *Ḥadīth*, *Kalām*, Astrology, Mathematics, Literature, History and Astronomy. He also studied Greek, Hebrew and Medicine. He came from a well-connected family, and his grandfather was a famous Mālikī jurist and Imām of the Great Mosque of Cordova.

Ibn Rushd lived through a change of dynasty within North Africa but remained a prominent jurist, eventually becoming the Chief Qāḍī of Cordova for twelve years.

In 578/1172 he became chief physician to Abū Ya'qūb Yūsuf, the Moroccan Sulṭān. At the death of Yūsuf he became physician and best friend to his successor al-Manṣūr, basing himself in Marrakesh, (Morocco).

During the reign of al-Manṣūr Ibn Rushd was accused by other scholars of being an apostate. Public opinion quickly turned against him and al-Manṣūr had no choice but to exile him to Cordova. However, the charges against him were eventually dismissed and he returned to Marrakesh and was reinstated in his job.

At the age of forty Ibn Rushd chose to confine his work to *Fiqh* and philosophy. However, his contribution to the medical field is significant. He wrote on smallpox and his medical works were used by subsequent generations, some of them being part of the curriculum within European universities.

By the 12th century most of Ibn Rushd's major work was translated into Latin, including his significant commentary on Aristotle. His impact on western academia is unparalleled and secures his place as a contributor to human knowledge.

On his return to Marrakesh from exile at the age of seventy, Ibn Rushd's health had deteriorated and he died shortly after in 595/1198.

Ibn-Rushd: The *Incoherence of the Incoherence [Tahāfut al-Tahāfut]*. Translated from Arabic by Simon Van de-Bergh. Cambridge: Gibb Memorial Trust, 1954.

Muṣliḥ al-Dīn Saʿdī

Shaykh Muṣliḥ al-Dīn Saʿdī was born in Persia in 1184 CE. Very little is known of his life and much of it is shrouded in legend and tales of miracles.

However, it is known that he was orphaned at a young age and raised by his elder brother. Until 1226 CE he remained a student, receiving a comprehensive education in the classical sciences as well as philosophy, geology and history.

He studied at some of the most prestigious schools, travelling as far as Baghdad in order to learn from prominent scholars. While in Baghdad he came under the influence of sufism. As an already strict follower of the *Sharīʿa*, Sufism offered a spiritual depth to his practices.

On completion of his formal studies Shaykh Saʿdī decided to travel. In 1226 CE he set out on a journey that would last thirty years and cover the length and breadth of the Muslim world and beyond. He travelled through Khurāsān, Tartar, the Punjab, Gujarat, Yemen, Ḥijāz, Abyssinia, Palestine, North Africa and the Levant, and his journeys were marked by adventure and variety that would challenge his ideas and perceptions.

During his time in Jerusalem he spent periods in solitude and meditation, and while in Damascus he took on a lecturing position. His fame as a teacher and guide spread at a phenomenal rate. He also, at times, took part in jihād alongside the local people and at one point was captured by Frankish soldiers and shipped to Tripoli as a prisoner. He was sent into hard labour and remained there until a friend bought his freedom.

Once free Shaykh Saʿdī travelled to Shīrāz where he lived a relatively reclusive life, spending his days writing or in meditation. During this time he wrote his famous works *Gulistān* and *Bustān*. Remarkably Shaykh Saʿdī was already at the age of eighty when he completed these two magnificent pieces of literature.

It is not clear when Saʿdī passed away, however the most commonly accepted view is that he died at the grand age of one hundred and ten in the year 1291 CE.

Shaykh Saʿdī's literature offers Muslim and non-Muslim readers a source for spiritual awakening and growth.

Shaykh Muṣliḥ al-Dīn Saʿdī: *The Rose Garden [The Gulistān].* Translated from Arabic by Edward B. Eastwick. London: The Octagon Press Ltd, 1979.

Muḥammad Ibn Idrīs Al-Shāfiʿī

Muḥammad Ibn Idrīs Al-Shāfiʿī was born in Gaza in 150/767. His father died while he was still a young child and his mother subsequently raised him.

As a student he memorised the Qur'ān and followed traditional lines of study. At the age of twenty he travelled to Madīna to study under Imām Mālik. There he spent his time learning from the great jurist and remained his devout student until the Imām's death in 179/796. At the time of Imām Mālik's death Imām Shāfiʿī had already developed reputation as a competent jurist.

At the age of thirty Imām Shāfiʿī was appointed a jurist by the governor of Yemen. During his time in Yemen he became entangled in local and fractional disputes and was eventually dismissed from his post and arrested. He was taken in chains to Iraq in the year 187/803 to face charges; however in the court of Hārūn al-Rashīd, Imām Shāfiʿī was cleared. On his release he chose to withdraw from public life and instead studied Ḥanafī *fiqh* intensively. Eventually he returned to Makka, via Syria in 188/804.

In Makka he took up a teaching position within the compound of the Holy Mosque and impressed his students with his profound knowledge of Islamic jurisprudence. His teaching left a lasting impression on Aḥmad ibn Ḥanbal and influenced his later theological opinions.

In 198/814 Imām Shāfiʿī migrated to Cairo, Egypt after a short return to Baghdad. In Cairo he continued teaching and entered his most prolific time in writing.

After a considerably difficult public life and career, Imām Shāfiʿī spent his final years in relative peace, managing to refine and improve his juristic theories away from the political influences of his time. He died in Cairo in the year 204 / 820 at the age of fifty-four and was buried there.

The contribution of Imām Shāfiʿī to Islamic juristic knowledge is exceptional. His work formed the backbone of all future juristic discourse and he is considered one of the forefathers of Islamic jurisprudence.

Majid Khadduri: *Al-Shāfʿi's Risāla – Treatise on the Foundations of Islamic Jurisprudence.* Cambridge: Islamic Texts Society, 1987.

Ibn Sīnā

Abū ʿAlī al-Ḥusayn ibn ʿAbdullāh ibn Sīnā, also known by his Latin name Avicenna, was born in 370/980 in Aṣfahān, in present day Uzbekistan.

Ibn Sīnā received his initial education at home from his father, and at the age of ten had memorised the whole of the Qur'ān. From there he attended the classes of the famous philosopher Abū ʿAbdullāh al-Nātilī, studying Philosophy, Greek and Muslim Logic. Ibn Sīnā's skill and sharp mind was apparent from an early age and it has been reported that it was he that explained the full depth of logic to his teacher Nātilī.

At thirteen he began to study medicine and not long after mastered the practice. By sixteen he was treating patients and being consulted by other physicians. At the age of seventeen ibn Sīnā cured Sulṭān Manṣūr of an illness that had escaped the knowledge and medical experience of prominent physicians of the time. When asked to request his desired reward, he asked simply for the use of the Royal Library.

On the death of his father ibn Sīnā spent some years travelling around Khurāsān and worked as a teacher, physician, administrator and jurist. Eventually, he settled in Ḥamadān in west-central Iran and worked as a court physician. It was here that he wrote his medical encyclopaedia *al-Qānūn fi'l-Ṭibb*, known also by its Latin title *Canon*.

The contribution this book made to the medical field cannot be underestimated. It was continuously used for over six centuries as a medical reference book within the Muslim and non-Muslim world. During the last thirty years of the 15th century the *Canon* was issued sixteen times, fifteen of which were in Latin and one in Hebrew. It was also reissued more than twenty times during the 16th century.

Ibn Sīnā's philosophical work and commentary on Aristotle evoked criticism by his peers and some even accused him of apostasy. On occasions he was imprisoned by princes and governors and in other instances those same princes would publicly honour him. Ultimately, political instability and agendas influenced how well his work was received and this continued, to a certain extent, after his death.

He spent the last years of his life in relative peace and died in Ḥamadān at the age of fifty-seven.

Ibn Sina: *Avicenna on Theology.* Translated from Arabic by A.J. Arberry. London: John Murray, 1951.

Ibn al-Ḥusayn al-Sulamī

Abū ʿAbd al-Raḥmān Muḥammad ibn al-Ḥusayn al-Sulamī was born in 325/936 in Nishapur, in present-day Iran.

After the completion of his formal studies Sulamī spent time travelling the Muslim world and seeking out respected teachers and thinkers. By 386/996 many Sufis felt that the mystical order was in decline and a new look at the role of Sufism in orthodox religion was considered necessary. Generally it was believed that a wide and difficult gap existed between orthodox and Sufi interpretations of the religion, and this divide had resulted in violent outbreaks in the past.

Sulamī ranks amongst ʿAbd al-Qādir Jīlānī and Imām Ghazālī in his attempts to bridge this divide. In his work he sought to produce a union between *Sharīʿa* and Sufism, seeing Sufism as the inner dimension of outer obedience. Thus, when used together in the worship of God, *Sharīʿa* and Sufism were considered as complementary of each other, and Sulamī believed harmonisation of the two would benefit both schools of thought and the individual Muslim. Later his student Qushayrī would continue in this mission and also establish himself as a respected teacher.

Al-Sulamī died in 412/1021 in his home town of Nishapur at the age of eighty-five.

Ibn al-Ḥusayn al-Sulamī: *The Book of Sufi Chivalry.* Translated from Arabic by Sheikh Tosun Bayrak al-Jerrahi al-Halveh. London: East-West Publications, 1983.

Al-Suyūṭī

Jalāl al-Dīn ʿAbd al-Raḥmān ibn Abī Bakr al-Suyūṭī was born in Asyūṭ in Upper Egypt, in 848/1445 His ancestry was originally from Persia and Turkey.

Al-Suyūṭī's education was broad-based and included not only the traditional subjects such as *tafsīr*, *ḥadīth* and *fiqh*, but also history, philosophy and rhetoric.

Eventually the young student moved to Cairo where he continued his education at the renowned Al-Azhar University. On completion of his studies he became part of the teaching staff and was subsequently promoted to Head Professor.

Al-Suyūṭī continued in this role, contributing to the academic progress of the university until 1501 CE, when he was accused by opponents of misuse of university funds. He chose to resign from his position rather than face the allegations and moved to the lonely Nile island of Rawḍa. There, he lived in relative seclusion and devoted his time and energy to writing.

Al-Suyūṭī died on the island after only four years of voluntary seclusion in 911/1505 at the age of sixty. His books are said to number over five hundred, and what he left for future generations in fields such as philosophy, history, medicine and theology has made an important contribution to Muslim knowledge and learning.

As-Suyuti: *Medicine of the Prophet.* Translated from Arabic by Ahmad Thompson. London: Taha Publishers Ltd, 1994.

Al-Ṭabarī

Abū Jaʿfar Muḥammad ibn Jarīr al-Ṭabarī was born in 224/838 in Amul, the capital city of Tabaristan near the Caspian Sea.

At the tender age of twelve Ṭabarī was sent to al-Ray, present day Tehran, to learn from some of the most prestigious scholars of his time.

Five years passed and the urge to travel and learn arose, so he made his way to Baghdad and later Kūfa.

In 244/858 Ṭabarī found himself back in Baghdad as a student. During this period he experienced bouts of poverty and on occasion was forced to sell his clothing and possessions to make ends meet. He eventually continued his travels to Syria, Egypt, Palestine and present day Lebanon, seeking out the established scholars of those regions, and after some time he completed the pilgrimage to Makka and returned to Baghdad.

While living in Baghdad he spent his time in teaching and writing and repeatedly refused government and judicial positions, choosing instead to concentrate on scholarly work. Ṭabarī developed good relations with his neighbours and would attend picnics and advise them on the upbringing of their children. However, he chose to remain celibate, as he felt domestic life would only distract him from what he felt was his calling.

His famous work *Ta'rīkh* charts the history of man from the Prophet Adam's time to Ṭabarī's, and rather than simply supply a factual account of events, it seeks to reveal the plan of God through an exploration of events, their causes and consequences. Within Baghdad society Ṭabarī's role as a teacher and spokesman was also invaluable.

He died in the year 310/ 923 at the age of eighty-five.

Al-Ṭabarī: *The History of al-Ṭabarī [Ta'rīkh al-Rusul wa'l-Mulūk – Vol 1*]. Translated from Arabic by Franz Rosenthal. New York: State University of New York Press, 1989.

Ibn Taymiyya

Taqī al-Dīn Abu'l-ʿAbbās Aḥmad ibn ʿAbdullāh ibn Taymiyya was born in Ḥarrān in modern day northern Syria and Iraq in the year 661/1263.

He was raised in troubled times and eventually the family fled their home and settled in Damascus when Ibn Taymiyya was seven years old.

As a young student he studied both secular and religious sciences, and at the age of twenty began teaching and also debating with the various theologians and philosophers within Damascus. He soon developed a name for himself as a deep thinker and competent debater, but as his reputation grew, Ibn Taymiyya drew the attention of a wide range of thinkers and soon a small group emerged as opponents to his theological arguments. On a number of occasions his enemies accused him of holding blasphemous beliefs and sought to have him imprisoned.

Between 699 and 702 AH Damascus was a city under siege where people lived in permanent fear of the Tartar invasion, many fleeing their homes and livelihoods in search of security. Ibn Taymiyya chose to stay and played an active part in encouraging the population to remain within the city gates and prepare to fight off the invasion.

Soon after the military threat was permanently removed, Ibn Taymiyya returned to teaching and actively fought against innovative behaviour amongst the Muslims of the city. Again his enemies banded together to work against him and in 705/1307 Taymiyya was ordered to go to Egypt to face charges. He was found guilty by the court and imprisoned, along with his two brothers and numerous followers.

On his release in 712/1313 Ibn Taymiyya returned to Damascus and was given a hero's welcome. His opponents again worked hard to discredit him during this period and successfully had him imprisoned on two or three more occasions. In 726/1326 he was arrested and put into the citadel of Damascus, where he was denied the use of a pen and paper and his books were confiscated.

In 728/1328 at the age of sixty-seven, while still in the citadel, Ibn Taymiyya was taken ill and died soon after. His death sent shock waves through the city, with an estimated 60,000 to 100,000 mourners followed his funeral procession.

Ibn Taymiyyah: *Letters from Prison.* Translated from Arabic by Muhammad Al-Abdah. Hounslow: Message of Islam UK, 1998.

Ibn Taymiyyah: *Al-Ubudiyyah – Being a True Slave of Allah.* London: Taha Publishers Ltd, 1999.

Fāṭima al-Zahra

Fāṭima al-Zahra was the fifth child of the Prophet Muḥammad (peace be upon him). Her mother was the Prophet's first wife Khadīja and Fāṭima was born during the time that Muḥammad spent lengthy periods in solitude meditating in the mountains around Makka.

Revelation began when Fāṭima was at the young age of five and she grew up witnessing the persecution of the Prophet Muḥammad (peace be upon him) and his followers by Quraysh.

Soon after she lost her beloved mother Khadīja, leaving her not only with a deep sense of grief, but also a greater responsibility to her father. She took it upon herself to ensure that her father was looked after, to the point where she became known as Umm Abīhā (mother of her father). The relationship between father and daughter grew stronger over the years and was characterised by admiration, love and respect.

She migrated to Madīna soon after her father and continued to live with him in his household. Later she married ʿAlī ibn Abī Ṭālib. Their home life was characterised by hardship and little provision, which they endured with patience, and acceptance of God's will.

Fāṭima al-Zahra and ʿAlī ibn Abī Ṭālib had four children, two boys and two girls.

Her two sons, Al-Ḥasan and Al-Ḥusayn, emerged within Islamic history as two important and influential figures and one of her daughters became known as the 'Heroine of Karbalā".

During the Battle of Uḥud and the Battle of the Trench, Fāṭima al-Zahra actively took part in the war effort and provided crucial support to the fighting army.

She also travelled to Makka with the Prophet and Muslims, thus witnessing the groundbreaking Treaty of Ḥudaybīyah and the peaceful conquest of Makka.

Soon after the return to Madīna, Muḥammad (peace be upon him) took ill and died in the house of his wife ʿĀ'isha.

Grief overtook the community and Fāṭima al-Zahra was no exception. The loss of the Prophet, her father, took its toll and she died soon after. She was the first amongst his family to join him in the next life as predicted by the Prophet himself.

May Allah, the Most High, be well pleased with all the Companions of the Messenger of Allah (peace be upon him) and be merciful to those that followed them. Amen.

Bibliography

Mohammed Abdul-Rauf: *Bilal Ibn-Rabah, A Leading Companion of the Prophet Muhammad.* U.S.A: American Trust Publications, 1977.

M. Adil: *Letters of Hazrat Umar Farooq*. Karachi: International Islamic Publishers Ltd, 1987.

Syed Rizwan Ali: *Sultan al-Ulama al-Izzedin Ibn Abdussalam: A Great Muslim Jurist & Reformer of the 13th Century AD.* New Delhi: Adam Publishers & Distributors, 1999.

Roland Boradhurst: *The Travels of Ibn-Jubayr*. London: Goodward Books, 1952.

Assad Nimer Busool: *Forty Hadith on the Importance of Knowledge, Learning and Teaching*. New Delhi: Goodwood Books, 2002.

Assad Nimer Busool: *Bouquet of the Noble Hadith, 240 Hadith on Fada'il*. New Delhi: Goodwood Books, 2002.

Ibn Rajab al-Ḥanbalī: *The Heirs of the Prophet*. Translated from Arabic by Zaid Shakir. Illinois: Starlatch Press, 2001.

Syed Masood Ul-Hasan: *110 Ahadith Qudsi, Sayings of the Prophet Having Allah's Statements.* Riyadh: Darussalam, 2003.

Majid Ali Khan: The Pious Caliphs. Kuala Lumpar: The Islamic Book Trust.

Abū'l-Ḥasan Al-Mārwadī: *The Laws of Islamic Governance [Al-Aḥkām As-Sulṭāniyyah]*. Translated from Arabic by Dr. Asadullah Yate. London: Taha Publishers Ltd, 1996.

Abul Hasan Ali Nadwi: *Saviours of Islamic Spirit, Vol I.* Karachi: Darul Ishaat, 1994.

Seyyed Hossein Nasr: Three *Muslim Sages: Avicenna, Suhrawardi, Ibn ʿArabī.* Massachusetts: Harvard University Press, 1964.

Ibn Saʿid*: Moorish Poetry; A Translation of The Pennants of the Champions and the Standards of the Distinguished.* London: Cambridge University Press, 1953.

Jalal Ad-Din Al-Suyuti: *The History of the Khalifahs Who Took the Right Way.* London: Taha Publishers Ltd, 1995.

Muhammad Abu Zahra: *The Four Imams; Their Lives, Works and Schools of Thought*. London: Dar al-Taqwa, 2001.

Abdul-Lateef Az-Zubaidi: The *Translation of the Meaning of Summarized Sahih Al-Bukhari*. Translated by Dr Muhammed Muhsin Khan. Saudi Arabia: Maktaba Dar-us-Salam, 1994.

Notes and References

Introduction

1. Imām al-Ghazālī: *The Ninety-Nine Beautiful Names of God.* Translated with notes by David B. Burrel and Nazih Daher. Cambridge: The Islamic Text Society, 1992, p.1.
2. Muhammad Asad: *The Meaning of the Qur'ān*, 40: 67.
3. Al-Junayd: *The Life, Personality and Writings of al-Junayd.* (Dr. Ali Hassan Abdul Kadir.) London: Luzac and Company Ltd, 1962.
4. Ibn ʿArabī: *Journey to the Lord of Power.* Translated by Rabia Terry Harris. London: East-West Publications Ltd, 1981.

I. The Self
1. Reflection

5. *Ḥadīth* (Tirmidhī).
6. Sayyid Quṭb: *In the Shade of the Qur'ān.* London: MWH Publishers, 1979, p77.
7. Shaykh ʿAbd al-Qādir Al-Jīlānī: *Jilā' al-Khāṭir (Purification of the Mind).* Edited by Sheikh Muhammad al-Casazani al-Husseini and translated by Prof. Shetha al-Dargazelli and Dr. Louay Fatoohi. Kuala Lumpur: A.S.Noordeen, 1999, p.137.

8. Syed Ruzee: *Nahjul Balagha; Sermons, Letters and Sayings of Hazrat Ali*. Translated by Syed Mohammed Askari Jafery. India: Seerat-u-Zahra Committee, 1965, p.461.
9. Here Abū Madyan relays, in simple but powerful terms, the fact that through reflection on who we are and what we do we can begin to recognise our faults, internal and external, and consequently be in control of our desires, inclinations and actions.
10. Vincent. J. Cornell: *The Way of Abū Madyan – The Works of Abū Madyan*. Cambridge: The Islamic Text Society, 1996, p.126.
11. Sayyid Quṭb: *In the Shade of the Qur'ān*. London: MWH Publishers, 1979, p.123.
12. Shaykh ʿAbd al-Qādir al-Jīlānī: *The Removal of Cares [Jalā' al-Khawāṭir – A Collection of Forty Discourses.]* Translated by Muhtar Holland. Fort Lauderdale: Al-Baz Publishing Inc, 1997. p. 245.
13. In this parable Shaykh Saʿdī beautifully illustrates how contemplation and reflection can lead the individual to higher states of consciousness so that he/she loses all sense of him/herself and becomes immersed in the new revelation.
14. Shaykh Muṣliḥ al-Dīn Saʿdī: *The Gulistān [Rose Garden]*. Translated by Edward B Eastwick. London: The Octagon Press Ltd, 1979, p.4.
15. The principle here is that failing to fully comprehend a reality is in itself a realisation. Thus, realising the limitations of our hearts and minds in the search of knowledge and wisdom is a level of awareness, and recognition of the omnipotent nature of God.
16. Jalal Al-Din Al-Suyuti: *The History of the Khalifahs Who Took the Right Way*. London: Taha Publishers Ltd, 1995, p.98.

2. Knowledge

17. *Ḥadīth* (Al-Ṭabarānī).
18. Shaykh ʿAbd al-Qādir Al-Jīlānī: *Jilā' al-Khāṭir [Purification of the Mind]*. Edited by Sheikh Muhammad al-Casazani al-Husseini and translated by Prof. Shetha al-Dargazelli and Dr. Louay Fatoohi. Kuala Lumpur: A.S.Noordeen, 1999, p.7.

19. Ibn Rajab al-Ḥanbalī: *The Heirs of the Prophet*. Translated by Zaid Shakir) Illinois: Starlatch Press, 2001, pp 55-56.
20. The metaphor of learning as rain, the learner searching for the rain cloud and waiting patiently under it alludes to the essential nature of knowledge for our existence. Thus, like the air we breathe and the water we need to survive, without knowledge we die spiritually and intellectually. Furthermore, through the search and acquisition of knowledge and wisdom we remove the shackles of this world and achieve a higher state of contentment and freedom.
21. Dr Ali Hassan Abdul Kadir: *The Life, Personality and Writing of al-Junayd*. London: Luzac & Company Ltd, 1962, p.138.
22. Muhammad Abu Zahra: *The Four Imams: Their Lives, Works and their Schools of Thought*. London: Dar al-Taqwa, 2001, p.32.
23. Ibid, p.275.
24. Ibn Rajab al-Ḥanbalī: *The Heirs of the Prophet*. Translated by Zaid Shakir. Illinois: Starlatch Press, 2001, p.40.
25. Knowledge of God involves the realisation that His essential nature is beyond human understanding. Questions of how and where He exists are nonsensical because God is not subject to the same physical limitations as creation.
26. Dr Ali Hassan Abdul Kadir: *The Life, Personality and Writing of al-Junayd*. London: Luzac & Company Ltd, 1962, p.171.
27. This leads on from the previous quote in that it further describes our inability to know the true nature of God and that the realisation of this fact is in itself an acquisition of wisdom. Thus, knowing that we don't know is knowledge.
28. Imām al-Ghazālī: *The Ninety-Nine Beautiful Names of God*. Translated with notes by David B. Burrel and Nazih Daher. Cambridge: The Islamic Text Society, 1992, p.42.
29. Ibid: p.117.
30. Ibid: p.117.
31. Shaykh Muṣliḥ al-Dīn Saʿdī: *The Gulistān [Rose Garden]*. Translated by Edward B Eastwick) London: The Octagon Press Ltd, 1979, p.207.

32. *Ḥadīth* (Tirmidhī).
33. Although knowing ourselves and knowing God are interlinked, we create our own barriers to self-awareness. Whereas, the limitations of knowing God exist because of His different nature to creatures and our hindering desire to search for God in ourselves.
34. Dr Ali Hassan Abdul Kadir: *The Life, Personality and Writing of al-Junayd.* London: Luzac & Company Ltd, 1962, p.175.
35. Imām al-Ghazālī: *On Disciplining the Soul and Breaking the Two Desires [Iḥyā' 'Ulūm al-Dīn].* Translated by T.J. Winter. Cambridge: The Islamic Text Society, 1995, p24.
36. Abū'l-Qāsim al-Qushayarī: *Sufi Book of Spiritual Ascent [Al-Risāla Al-Qushayriyya].* Translated by Rabia Harris. Chicago: Kazi Publications, 1997, p.21.
37. Imām al-Ghazālī: *The Book of Destructive Evils – Volume III, Book of Worldly Usages [Iḥyā' 'Ulūm al-Dīn].* Translated by Al-Haj Maulana Fazlul Karim. Delhi: Islamic Book Service, 1982, p.66.
38. Shaykh 'Abd al-Qādir al-Jīlānī: *The Removal of Cares [Jalā' al-Khawāṭir – A Collection of Forty Discourses].* Translated by Muhtar Holland. Fort Lauderdale: Al-Baz Publishing Inc, 1997. p. 279.
39. Imām al-Ghazālī: *On Disciplining the Soul and Breaking the Two Desires [Iḥyā' 'Ulūm al-Dīn].* Translated by T.J. Winter. Cambridge: The Islamic Text Society, 1995, p.57.
40. Ibn Ḥazm al-Andalusī: *In Pursuit of Virtue.* London: Taha Publishers, 1990, p.7.
41. Prof. Shibli Numani: *Al-Farooq, The Life of Omar the Great - Second Caliph of Islam.*.Translated by Maulana Zafar Ali Khan. New Delhi: International Islamic Publishers, 1992, p.442.
42. Jalal Al-Din Al-Suyuti: *The History of the Khalifahs Who Took the Right Way.* London: Taha Publishers Ltd, 1995, p.98.

4. Whims and Desires

43. *Ḥadīth* (Ṣaḥīḥ al-Jāmi' al-Ṣaghīr).

44. This quote points to the importance of conquering our basic whims and urges. It highlights that through overcoming our passions and attachments to this world we move beyond the harm of creatures and become protected from any sense of loss, since we have voluntarily abandoned our love for worldly things.
45. Imām al-Ghazālī: *The Ninety-Nine Beautiful Names of God.* Translated with notes by David B. Burrel and Nazih Daher Cambridge: The Islamic Text Society, 1992, p.74.
46. Abul Hasan Ali Nadwi: *Saviours of Islamic Spirit, Volume I.* Karachi: Darul Ishaat, 1994, p.42.
47. Shaykh ʿAbd al-Qādir Al-Jīlānī: *Jilā' al-Khāṭir (Purification of the Mind).* Edited by Sheikh Muhammad al-Casazani al-Husseini and translated by Prof. Shetha al-Dargazelli and Dr. Louay Fatoohi. Kuala Lumpur: A.S.Noordeen, 1999, p.15.
48. Imām al-Ghazālī: *The Ninety-Nine Beautiful Names of God.* Translated with notes by David B. Burrel and Nazih Daher. Cambridge: The Islamic Text Society, 1992, p.82.
49. Syed Ruzee: *Nahjul Balagha; Sermons, Letters and Sayings of Hazrat Ali.* Translated by Syed Mohammed Askari Jafery. India: Seerat-u-Zahra Committee, 1965, p.187.
50. Sayyid Quṭb: *In the Shade of the Qur'ān.* London: MWH Publishers, 1979, p.33.
51. The simple but profound point is made that an inclination or desire towards something can lead an individual to become absorbed in the thing which he/she craves, if left unchecked. Therefore, before imparting this simple fact to others the individual must first learn it through self-awareness and control.
52. Charles Upton: *'Doorkeeper of the Heart, Versions of Rabiʿa*, Vermont, Threshold Books, 1988, p.39.

5. Sincerity

53. *Ḥadīth.*
54. Sheikh ʿAbd al-Qādir Al-Jīlānī: *Jilā' al-Khāṭir (Purification of the Mind)*, (Edited by Sheikh Muhammad al-Casazani al-Husseini

and translated by Prof. Shetha al-Dargazelli and Dr. Louay Fatoohi) Kuala Lumpur: A.S.Noordeen, 1999, p. 42.

55. Abū'l-Qāsim al-Qushayrī: *Sufi Book of Spiritual Ascent [Al-Risāla Al-Qushayriyya]*. Translated by Rabia Harris. Chicago: Kazi Publications, 1997, p.173.
56. Vincent. J. Cornell: *The Way of Abū Madyan – The Works of Abū Madyan*. Cambridge: The Islamic Text Society, 1996, p.138.
57. Ibn Taymiyyah: *Al-ʿUbudiyyah – Being a True Slave of Allah*. London: Taha Publishers Ltd, 1999, p. 120.
58. The metaphor here illustrates that while a believer's actions may change during the course of his/her life, sincerity to God must not change and all choices must be built on a sound foundation of faith.
59. Muhtar Holland: *Utterances of Sheikh Abd al-Qadir al-Jilani*. Fort Lauderdale: Al-Baz Publishers Inc, 1998, p.55.
60. Abū'l-Qāsim al-Qushayrī: *Sufi Book of Spiritual Ascent [Al-Risāla Al-Qushayriyya]*. Translated by Rabia Harris) Chicago: Kazi Publications, 1997, p.177.

6. Patience

61. *Ḥadīth* (Bukhārī and Muslim).
62. During the time of 'The Slander'
63. Vincent. J. Cornell: *The Way of Abū Madyan – The Works of Abū Madyan*. Cambridge: The Islamic Text Society, 1996, p.120.
64. Shaykh ʿAbd al-Qādir Al-Jīlānī: *Jilā' al-Khāṭir (Purification of the Mind)*. Edited by Sheikh Muhammad al-Casazani al-Husseini and translated by Prof. Shetha al-Dargazelli and Dr. Louay Fatoohi. Kuala Lumpur: A.S. Noordeen, 1999, p. 37.
65. Ibn Qayyim al-Jawziyya: *Implements for the Patient, Supplies for the Grateful – The Way to Patience and Gratitude [ʿUddat aṣ-Ṣābirīn wa Dhakhīrat ash-Shākirīn]*. Edited and Translated by Chanicka and Salma Cook. Al-Mansura: Umm al-Qura Publishers, 2000, p.351.

II. The Self and God

1. Freedom and Servitude

66. *Ḥadīth* (Ṣaḥīḥ Muslim).
67. Majid Khadduri: *Al-Shāfiʿī's Risāla – Treatise on the Foundations of Islamic Jurisprudence.* Cambridge: The Islamic Text Society, 1987, p.123.
68. Sayyid Quṭb: *In the Shade of the Qur'ān*. London: MWH Publishers, 1979, p.350.
69. Ibn Taymiyyah: *Al-ʿUbudiyyah – Being a True Slave of Allah.* London: Taha Publishers Ltd, 1999, p.62.
70. Abū'l-Qāsim al-Qushayrī: *Sufi Book of Spiritual Ascent [Al-Risāla Al-Qushayriyya]*. Translated by Rabia Harris. Chicago: Kazi Publications, 1997, p.189.
71. Vincent. J. Cornell: *The Way of Abū Madyan – The Works of Abū Madyan*. Cambridge: The Islamic Text Society, 1996, p.118.
72. *Qur'ān:* S30, V43.
73. Shaykh ʿAbd al-Qādir Al-Jīlānī: *Jilā' al-Khāṭir (Purification of the Mind.* Edited by Sheikh Muhammad al-Casazani al-Husseini and translated by Prof. Shetha al-Dargazelli and Dr. Louay Fatoohi. Kuala Lumpur: A.S. Noordeen, 1999, p.25.
74. The highest level of freedom is submission to God and His will for the believer. This also ultimately releases the individual to subservience to other creatures.
75. Abū'l-Qāsim al-Qushayrī: *Sufi Book of Spiritual Ascent [Al-Risāla Al-Qushayriyya]*. Translated by Rabia Harris) Chicago: Kazi Publications, 1997, p.190.

2. Closeness to God

76. *Ḥadīth Qudsī* (Bukhārī and Muslim).
77. Abū'l-Qāsim al-Qushayrī: *Sufi Book of Spiritual Ascent [Al-Risāla Al-Qushayriyya]*. Translated by Rabia Harris. Chicago: Kazi Publications, 1997, p.195.
78. Shaykh ʿAbd al-Qādir al-Jīlānī: *The Removal of Cares [Jalā' al-Khawāṭir – A Collection of Forty Discourses]*. Translated by Muhtar Holland. Fort Lauderdale: Al-Baz Publishing Inc, 1997. p. 113.

79. Shaykh ʿAbd al-Qādir Al-Jīlānī: *Jilā' al-Khāṭir (Purification of the Mind)*. Edited by Sheikh Muhammad al-Casazani al-Husseini and translated by Prof. Shetha al-Dargazelli and Dr. Louay Fatoohi. Kuala Lumpur: A.S. Noordeen, 1999, p.61.
80. Prof Masud ul-Hassan: *Ṣiddīq-l-Akbar, Ḥazrat Abū Bakr.* New Delhi: Kitab Bhavan, p.253.
81. While Rūmī encourages those that desire closeness to God to use all that is at their disposal to do so he gently advises the seeker to remain focussed on the ultimate goal of nearness to God, and to not become distracted on the way.
82. Reynold A Nicholson: *The Mathnawi of Jalalu'ddin Rumi.* New Delhi: Adam Publishers & Distributors, 1930, pp.56-57.

3. Remembrance

83. *Ḥadīth Qudsī* (Bukhārī).
84. Charles Upton: *Doorkeeper of the Heart, Versions of Rabiʿa.* Vermont, Threshold Books, 1988, p.25.
85. Ibn ʿAṭā' Allāh al-Iskandarī: *The Key to Salvation: A Sufi Manual.* Cambridge: The Islamic Text Society, 1996, p.45.
86. Abū'l-Qāsim al-Qushayrī: *Sufi Book of Spiritual Ascent [Al-Risāla Al-Qushayriyya]*. Translated by Rabia Harris. Chicago: Kazi Publications, 1997, p.196.
87. Ahmed Thompson: *As-Suyuti's Medicine of the Prophet.* London: Taha Publishers, 1994, p.199.
88. Ibn Taymiyyah: *Al-ʿUbudiyyah – Being a True Slave of Allah.* London: Taha Publishers Ltd, 1999, p. 84.
89. Ibn ʿArabī: *Journey to the Lord of Power [from Treatise on the Lights in the Secrets Granted to One Who Understands Retreat]*. Translated by Rabia Terri Harris. London, East-West Publications, 1981, p.31.
90. Ibn ʿAṭā' Allāh al-Iskandarī: *The Key to Salvation: A Sufi Manual.* Cambridge: The Islamic Text Society, 1996, p.75.
91. Ibid: p.45.

92. Ibid: p.45.
93. *Ḥadīth Qudsī* (Mālik ibn Anas in *Al-Muwaṭṭa'*).
94. Prof Masud ul-Hassan: *Ṣiddīq-l-Akbar, Ḥazrat Abū Bakr.* New Delhi: Kitab Bhavan.
95. The analogue of Majnūn and Laylā appears in various Sufi literatures to illustrate the desired stage of complete attention to, devotion and love for God.
96. Shaykh ʿAbd al-Qādir al-Jīlānī: *The Removal of Cares [Jalā' al-Khawāṭir – A Collection of Forty Discourses].* Translated by Muhtar Holland. Fort Lauderdale: Al-Baz Publishing Inc, 1997, p.12.
97. Ibn Taymiyyah: *Letters From Prison.* Translated by Muhammad Al-Abdah. Hounslow: Message of Islam, UK, 1998, p. 26.
98. Ibn Taymiyyah: *Al-ʿUbudiyyah – Being a True Slave of Allah.* London: Taha Publishers Ltd, 1999, p.88.
99. Ibn Qayyim al-Jawziyya: *Implements for the Patient, Supplies for the Grateful – The Way to Patience and Gratitude [ʿUddat uṣ-Ṣābirīn wa Dhakhīrat ash-Shākirīn].* Edited and Translated by Chanicka and Salma Cook. Al-Mansura: Umm al-Qura Publishers, 2000, p.366.

5. Fear

100. *Ḥadīth Qudsī* (Bukhārī and Muslim).
101. Al-Muqaddasī: *'Revelation of the Secrets of the Birds and Flowers'*, (Translated by Irene Hoare & Darya Galy) London: Octagon Press, 1979, p.45.
102. The Companions of the Prophet (peace be upon him) and those that followed them.
103. Imām al-Ghazālī: *The Remembrance of Death and the Afterlife [Iḥyā' ʿUlūm al-Dīn].* Translated by T.J. Winter. Cambridge: The Islamic Text Society, 1989, p.59.
104. Vincent. J. Cornell: *The Way of Abū Madyan – The Works of Abū Madyan.* Cambridge: The Islamic Text Society, 1996, p.122.
105. Shaykh ʿAbd al-Qādir Al-Jīlānī: *Jilā' al-Khāṭir (Purification of the Mind).* Edited by Sheikh Muhammad al-Casazani al-

Husseini and translated by Prof. Shetha al-Dargazelli and Dr. Louay Fatoohi. Kuala Lumpur: A.S. Noordeen, 1999, p.32.

106. Abū'l-Qāsim al-Qushayrī: *Sufi Book of Spiritual Ascent [Al-Risala Al-Qushayariyya]*. Translated by Rabia Harris. Chicago: Kazi Publications, 1997, p.53.
107. Shaykh ʿAbd al-Qādir Al-Jīlānī: *Jilā' al-Khāṭir (Purification of the Mind)*. Edited by Sheikh Muhammad al-Casazani al-Husseini and translated by Prof. Shetha al-Dargazelli and Dr. Louay Fatoohi. Kuala Lumpur: A.S. Noordeen, 1999, p.34.

6. Repentance

108. *Ḥadīth Qudsī* (Tirmidhī).
109. Reynold A Nicholson: *The Mathnawi of Jalalu'ddin Rumi*. New Delhi: Adam Publishers & Distributors, 1930, p.410.
110. Dr. Ahmed Zidan: *Revitalisation of the Sciences of Religion – Al-Ghazālī's Iḥyā' ʿUlūm al-Dīn.* Cairo: Islamic Inc. for Publishing and Distribution, 1997, p.220.
111. In this short poem Ibn ʿAbdun seeks repentance from God for wasted time and for falling victim to the illusion that time is always on our side.
112. A.J. Arberry: *Moorish Poetry*. London: Cambridge University Press, 1953, p.64.
113. Prophet Muḥammad (peace be upon him).
114. Vincent. J. Cornell: *The Way of Abū Madyan – The Works of Abū Madyan*. Cambridge: The Islamic Text Society, 1996, pp.40-46.

7. Humility

115. *Ḥadīth* (Muslim).
116. Prophet Yūsuf, upon him be peace.
117. Shaykh Muṣliḥ al-Dīn Saʿdī: *The Gulistān [Rose Garden]*. Translated by Edward B Eastwick. London: The Octagon Press Ltd, 1979, p.19.
118. Sheikh ʿAbd al-Qādir al-Jīlānī: *The Removal of Cares [Jalā' al-Khawāṭir – A Collection of Forty Discourses]*. Translated by Muhtar Holland. Fort Lauderdale: Al-Baz Publishing Inc, 1997, p.29.

119. *Ḥadīth.*
120. Ibn Qayyim al-Jawziyya: *Implements for the Patient, Supplies for the Grateful – The Way to Patience and Gratitude [ʿUddat aṣ-Ṣābirīn wa Dhakhīrat ash-Shākirin]*. Edited and Translated by Chanicka and Salma Cook. Al-Mansura: Umm al-Qura Publishers, 2000, p.367.
121. Vincent. J. Cornell: *The Way of Abū Madyan – The Works of Abū Madyan.* Cambridge: The Islamic Text Society, 1996, p.160.
122. Syed Ruzee: *Nahjul Balagha; Sermons, Letters and Sayings of Hazrat Ali.* Translated by Syed Mohammed Askari Jafery) India: Seerat-u-Zahra Committee, 1965, p.526.
123. Ibn Qayyim al-Jawziyya: *Implements for the Patient, Supplies for the Grateful – The Way to Patience and Gratitude [ʿUddat aṣ-Ṣābirīn wa Dhakhīrat ash-Shākirin]*. Edited and Translated by Chanicka and Salma Cook. Al-Mansura: Umm al-Qura Publishers, 2000, p.181.
124. Shaykh Muṣliḥ al-Dīn Saʿdī: *The Gulistān [Rose Garden]* Translated by Edward B Eastwick. London: The Octagon Press Ltd, 1979, p.2.

III. The Self and Mankind

1. Unity

125. *Ḥadīth* (Muslim and Bukhārī).
126. On arrival in Tunis city.
127. Ibn Juzayy: *Ibn Baṭṭūṭa; Travels in Africa and Asia.* London: Routledge & Kegan Paul, 1929, p.43.
128. As Ibn Baṭṭūta experienced himself when entering Tunis City, the Muslim character should be such that we respond to the needs of people around instinctively. Thus, aiding others is not dependent on requests for help.
129. Dr. Ahmed Zidan: *Revitalisation of the Sciences of Religion – Al-Ghazālī's Iḥyā' ʿUlūm al-Dīn.* Cairo: Islamic Inc. for Publishing and Distribution, 1997, p.257.

130. Ibn Khaldūn:*The Muqaddimah: An Introduction to History.* Translated by Franz Rosenthal. New York: Bollingen Foundation Inc, 1958, p.83.
131. Ibn Taymiyyah: *Letters From Prison.* Translated by Muhammad Al-Abdah. Hounslow: Message of Islam, UK, 1998, p.16.
132. Prof Masud ul-Hassan: *Ṣiddīq-l-Akbar, Ḥazrat Abū Bakr.* New Delhi: Kitab Bhavan. p.250.
133. Ibid; p.249.
134. Ibn al-Ḥusayn al-Sulamī: *The Book of Sufi Chivalry*. Translated by Sheikh Tosun Bayrak al-Jerrahi. London: East-West Publications, 1983, p.64.
135. On his deathbed (may God be well pleased with him).
136. Al-Ghazālī: *The Remembrance of Death and the Afterlife' [Iḥyā' 'Ulūm al-Dīn].* Translated by T.J. Winter. Cambridge: The Islamic Text Society, 1989, pp. 81-82.

2. Social and Political Affairs

137. *Ḥadīth* (al-Ṭabarānī).
138. Sayyid Quṭb: *Milestones.* The Holy Koran Publishing House, 1978, p.11.

139. A.J. Arberry, *Avicenna on Theology.* London: John Murry, 1951, p.42.
140. Abul Hasan Ali Nadwi: *Saviours of Islamic Spirit.* Karachi: Darul Ishaat, 1994, p.214.
141. On the commencement of his rule.
142. Prof Masud ul-Hassan: *Ṣiddīq-l-Akbar, Ḥazrat Abū Bakr.* New Delhi: Kitab Bhavan
143. Speaking as leader of the Muslims.
144. Al-Ghazālī: *The Kings.* Translated by F.R.C. Bagley. London: Oxford University Press, 1964, p.66.
145. Part of a circular letter sent to various governors of the state.
146. Abul Hasan Ali Nadwi: *Saviours of Islamic Spirit.* Karachi: Darul Ishaat, 1994, pp.32-33.
147. Said to his son al-Malik al-Ẓāhir, on his return from a journey.

148. Beha ed-Din Abu el-Mehasan: *The Life of Saladin 1137 – 1193 A.D.* New Delhi: Adam Publishers and Distributors, 1994, pp.392-393.
149. In a letter to the Governor of Egypt on hearing of him amassing wealth at the expense of the state treasury.
150. Dr. M Adil: *Letters of Hazrat Umar Farooq*, Karachi: International Islamic Publishers Ltd, 1987.
151. Shaykh Muṣliḥ al-Dīn Saʿdī: *The Gulistān [Rose Garden].* Translated by Edward B Eastwick. London: The Octagon Press Ltd, 1979, p.39.

3. Enjoining Good and Forbidding Evil

152. *Ḥadīth* (Muslim).
153. Muhtar Holland: *Utterances of Sheikh Abdul Qadir al-Jilani.* Fort Lauderdale: Al-Baz Publishing Inc. 1998, p.10.
154. Sayyid Quṭb: *Milestones.* The Holy Koran Publishing House, 1978, p.259.
155. Al-Ghazālī: *The Book of Religious Learning, Volume III; Book of Worldly Usages [Iḥyā' ʿUlūm al-Dīn].*Translated by Al-Haj Maulana Fazlil Karim. New Delhi: Islamic Book Service, 1991, p.202.
156. Prof. Shibli Numani: *Al-Farooq, The Life of Omar the Great - Second Caliph of Islam.* Translated by Maulana Zafar Ali Khan. New Delhi: International Islamic Publishers, 1992, p.442.
157. A.J. Arberry: *Moorish Poetry'* London: Cambridge University Press, 1953, pp.160-61.

4. Speech

158. *Ḥadīth* (Bukhārī and Tirmidhī).
159. Shaykh Muṣliḥ al-Dīn Saʿdī: *The Gulistān [Rose Garden].* Translated by Edward B Eastwick. London: The Octagon Press Ltd, 1979, p.11.
160. Al-Qushayrī independently comes to the same conclusion as Saʿdī (last quote) that silence and speech are of the same value. What makes one more worthy than the other is the

individual's choice of action: to remain silent or speak out. In some circumstances it would be nobler to speak while in others the opposite is also true.

161. Abū'l-Qāsim al-Qushayrī: *Sufi Book of Spiritual Ascent [Al-Risāla Al-Qushayriyya]*. Translated by Rabia Harris. Chicago: Kazi Publications, 1997, p.43.
162. Shaykh Muṣliḥ al-Dīn Sa'dī: *The Gulistān [Rose Garden]*. Translated by Edward B Eastwick. London: The Octagon Press Ltd, 1979, p.10.
163. Al-Ghazālī: *The Book of Religious Learning, Volume III; Book of Worldly Usages [Iḥyā' 'Ulūm al-Dīn]*. Translated by Al-Haj Maulana Fazlil Karim. New Delhi: Islamic Book Service, 1991, p.108.
164. Syed Ruzee: *Nahjul Balagha; Sermons, Letters and Sayings of Hazrat Ali*. Translated by Syed Mohammed Askari Jafery. India: Seerat-u-Zahra Committee, 1965, p.259.
165. Ibid, p.461.
166. Shaykh 'Abd al-Qādir al-Jīlānī: *The Removal of Cares [Jalā' al-Khawāṭir – A Collection of Forty Discourses.]* Translated by Muhtar Holland. Fort Lauderdale: Al-Baz Publishing Inc, 1997, p.225.
167. Ibn al-Ḥusayn al-Sulamī: *The Book of Sufi Chivalry*. Translated by Sheikh Tosun Bayrak al-Jerrahi. London: East-West Publications, 1983, p.56.
168. Shaykh 'Abd al-Qādir al-Jīlānī: *The Removal of Cares [Jalā' al-Khawāṭir – A Collection of Forty Discourses]*. Translated by Muhtar Holland. Fort Lauderdale: Al-Baz Publishing Inc, 1997, p.96.
169. Ibn Ḥazm al-Andalusī: *In Pursuit of Virtue*. London: Taha Publishers, 1990, p.127.

5. Friendship

170. *Ḥadīth* (Ṣaḥīḥ Muslim).
171. Charles Pellat: *The Life and Works of Jāḥiẓ*. Translated by D.M. Hawke. London: Routledge & Kegan Paul, 1969, p.222.

172. Shaykh ʿAbd al-Qādir Al-Jīlānī: *Jilā' al-Khāṭir (Purification of the Mind)*. Edited by Sheikh Muhammad al-Casazani al-Husseini and translated by Prof. Shetha al-Dargazelli and Dr. Louay Fatoohi. Kuala Lumpur: A.S. Noordeen, 1999, p.5.
173. Imām ʿAbdullāh ibn ʿAlawī al-Ḥaddād: *Knowledge and Wisdom*. Translated by Mostafa al-Badawi. Illinois: Starlatch Press, 2001, p.81.
174. Muhtar Holland: *Utterances of Sheikh Abdul Qadir al-Jilani*. Fort Lauderdale: Al-Baz Publishing Inc. 1998, p.75.
175. Shaykh ʿAbd al-Qādir al-Jīlānī: *The Removal of Cares [Jalā' al-Khawāṭir – A Collection of Forty Discourses]*. Translated by Muhtar Holland. Fort Lauderdale: Al-Baz Publishing Inc, 1997, p.42.
176. In this poem Abū ʿAmr highlights how an individual can be led astray through associating with bad company. He goes on to explain that an individual only needs to observe the effects of bad company on his/her character and conduct to become more aware of this fact.
177. A.J. Arberry; *Moorish Poetry*. London: Cambridge University Press, 1953, p.64.

178. Syed Ruzee: *Nahjul Balagha; Sermons, Letters and Sayings of Hazrat Ali*. Translated by Syed Mohammed Askari Jafery) India: Seerat-u-Zahra Committee, 1965, p.187.

6. Advice

179. *Ḥadīth* (Ṣaḥīḥ Muslim).
180. Prof Masud ul-Hassan: *Ṣiddīq-l-Akbar, Ḥazrat Abū Bakr.*, New Delhi: Kitab Bhavan, p.249.
181. Currency used in various Arab countries.
182. Reynold A Nicholson: *The Mathnawi of Jalalu'ddin Rumi*. New Delhi: Adam Publishers & Distributors, 1930, p.410.
183. Muhtar Holland: *Utterances of Sheikh Abdul Qadir al-Jilani*. Fort Lauderdale: Al-Baz Publishing Inc. 1998, p.82.

IV. The Self and the World

1. The World

184. *Ḥadīth* (Bukhārī).
185. Al-Ghazālī: *The Remembrance of Death and the Afterlife [Iḥyā' ʿUlūm al-Dīn]*. Translated by T.J. Winter. Cambridge: The Islamic Text Society, 1989, p.85.
186. Shaykh ʿAbd al-Qādir al-Jīlānī: *The Removal of Cares [Jalā' al-Khawāṭir – A Collection of Forty Discourses]*. Translated by Muhtar Holland. Fort Lauderdale: Al-Baz Publishing Inc, 1997, p.290.
187. Al-Muqaddasī: *Revelation of the Secrets of the Birds and Flowers*. Translated by Irene Hoare & Darya Galy. London: Octagon Press, 1979, p.68.
188. Shaykh ʿAbd al-Qādir Al-Jīlānī: *Jilā' al-Khāṭir (Purification of the Mind)*. Edited by Sheikh Muhammad al-Casazani al-Husseini and translated by Prof. Shetha al-Dargazelli and Dr. Louay Fatoohi. Kuala Lumpur: A.S. Noordeen, 1999, p.149.
189. Prof Masud ul-Hassan: *Ṣiddīq-l-Akbar, Ḥazrat Abu Bakr*. New Delhi: Kitab Bhavan, p.253.
190. Imām Abū Zakariyā al-Nawawī: *Riyāḍ al-Ṣāliḥīn*. Karachi: International Islamic Publishers, 1986: Introduction.
191. Syed Ruzee: *Nahjul Balagha; Sermons, Letters and Sayings of Hazrat Ali*. Translated by Syed Mohammed Askari Jafery. India: Seerat-u-Zahra Committee, 1965, p.166.
192. Reynold A Nicholson: *The Mathnawi of Jalalu'ddin Rumi*. New Delhi: Adam Publishers & Distributors, 1930, p.14.
193. Shaykh Muṣliḥ al-Dīn Saʿdī: *The Gulistān [Rose Garden]*. Translated by Edward B Eastwick. London: The Octagon Press Ltd, 1979, p.24.
194. Muhtar Holland: *Utterances of Sheikh Abdul Qadir al-Jilani*. Fort Lauderdale: Al-Baz Publishing Inc. 1998, p.70.

2. Actions

195. Ḥadīth Qudsī (Muslim).
196. To King Negus of Abyssinia.

197. Safi-ur-Rahman al-Mubarakpuri: *Ar-Raheeq Al-Makhtum [The Sealed Nectar]*. Riyadh: Maktaba Dar-us-Salam, 1995, p.103.
198. Ibn Kathīr: *Tafsīr Al-Qur'ān*. London: Al-Firdous Ltd, 1996, p.30.
199. Shaykh ʿAbd al-Qādir Al-Jīlānī: *Jilā' al-Khāṭir (Purification of the Mind)*. Edited by Sheikh Muhammad al-Casazani al-Husseini and translated by Prof. Shetha al-Dargazelli and Dr. Louay Fatoohi. Kuala Lumpur: A.S. Noordeen, 1999, p.54.
200. Imām ʿAbdullāh ibn ʿAlawī al-Ḥaddād: *Knowledge and Wisdom*. Translated by Mostafa al-Badawi. Illinois: Starlatch Press, 2001, p.27.
201. Ibid, p.79.
202. Abū'l-Qāsim al-Qushayrī: *Sufi Book of Spiritual Ascent [Al-Risāla Al-Qushayriyya]*. Translated by Rabia Harris. Chicago: Kazi Publications, 1997, p.169.
203. Imām ʿAbdullāh ibn ʿAlawī al-Ḥaddād: *Knowledge and Wisdom*. Translated by Mostafa al-Badawi. Illinois: Starlatch Press, 2001, p.25.
204. M.Saghir Hassan Maʿsumi: *Imām Rāzī's ʿIlm al-Akhlāq, The Book of Soul and Spirit and an Exposition of Their Faculties*. Pakistan: Islamic Research Institute, p.215.
205. Ibn Qayyim al-Jawziyya, *The Invocation of God*. London: The Islamic Text Society, 2000, p.15.
206. Syed Ruzee: *Nahjul Balagha; Sermons, Letters and Sayings of Hazrat Ali*. Translated by Syed Mohammed Askari Jafery. India: Seerat-u-Zahra Committee, 1965, p.527.
207. Ibid: p.193.

3. Provisions

208. *Ḥadīth Qudsī* (Musnad Aḥmad)
209. Franz Rosenthal: *The History of al-Ṭabarī [Ta'rīkh al-Rusul wa'l Mulūk –Volume I]*. New York: State University of New York Press, 1989, p.166.
210. Shaykh ʿAbd al-Qādir al-Jīlānī: *The Removal of Cares [Jalā' al-Khawāṭir – A Collection of Forty Discourses]*. Translated by

Muhtar Holland. Fort Lauderdale: Al-Baz Publishing Inc, 1997, p.132.

211. Shaykh Muṣliḥ al-Dīn Saʿdī: *The Gulistān [Rose Garden].* Translated by Edward B Eastwick. London: The Octagon Press Ltd, 1979, p.228.
212. Lieut-Col H Wilberforce Clarke: *The Divan-i-Hafiz,* Volume I & II. New York: Samuel Weiser Inc, 1989, pp.37-38.
213. Shaykh ʿAbd al-Qādir Al-Jīlānī: *Jilā' al-Khāṭir (Purification of the Mind).* Edited by Sheikh Muhammad al-Casazani al-Husseini and translated by Prof. Shetha al-Dargazelli and Dr. Louay Fatoohi. Kuala Lumpur: A.S. Noordeen, 1999, p.131.

4. Work

214. *Ḥadīth* (Al-Bukhārī).
215. Shaykh ʿAbd al-Qādir al-Jīlānī: *The Removal of Cares [Jalā' al-Khawāṭir – A Collection of Forty Discourses.]* Translated by Muhtar Holland. Fort Lauderdale: Al-Baz Publishing Inc, 1997, p.68.
216. Dr. Ahmed Zidan: *Revitalisation of the Sciences of Religion – Al-Ghazālī's Iḥyā' ʿUlūm al-Dīn.* Cairo: Islamic Inc. for Publishing and Distribution, 1997, pp237-238.
217. Ibn al-Ḥusayn al-Sulamī: *The Book of Sufi Chivalry.* Translated by Sheikh Tosun Bayrak al-Jerrahi. London: East-West Publications, 1983, p.44.
218. Ibn Khaldūn: *The Muqaddimah: An Introduction to History'.* Translated by Franz Rosenthal. New York: Bollingen Foundation Inc, 1958.p.104.
219. Ibid: p.124.

5. Hardship

220. *Ḥadīth* (Bukhārī and Muslim).
221. Ibn ʿArabī: *Journey to the Lord of Power'.* Translated by Rabia Terry Harris. London: East-West Publications Ltd, 1981, p.27.

222. Imām ʿAbdullāh ibn ʿAlawī al-Ḥaddād: *Knowledge and Wisdom*. Translated by Mostafa al-Badawi. Illinois: Starlatch Press, 2001, p.46.
223. M.Saghir Hassan Maʿsumi: *Imām Rāzī's ʿIlm al-Akhlāq; The Book of Soul and Spirit and an Exposition of Their Faculties*. Pakistan: Islamic Research Institute, p.182.
224. Shaykh ʿAbd al-Qādir Al-Jīlānī: *Jilā' al-Khāṭir (Purification of the Mind)*. Edited by Sheikh Muhammad al-Casazani al-Husseini and translated by Prof. Shetha al-Dargazelli and Dr. Louay Fatoohi. Kuala Lumpur: A.S. Noordeen, 1999, p.6.
225. Majid Khadduri: *Al-Shāfiʿī's Risāla – Treatise on the Foundations of Islamic Jurisprudence*. Cambridge: The Islamic Text Society, 1987, p.66.

6. Death

226. *Ḥadīth Qudsī* (Bukhārī).
227. Shaykh ʿAbd al-Qādir Al-Jīlānī: *Jilā' al-Khāṭir (Purification of the Mind)*. Edited by Sheikh Muhammad al-Casazani al-Husseini and translated by Prof. Shetha al-Dargazelli and Dr. Louay Fatoohi. Kuala Lumpur: A.S. Noordeen, 1999, p.178.
228. Munkar and Nakīr: Angels that question the dead in the grave.
229. Al-Ghazālī: *The Remembrance of Death and the Afterlife [Iḥyā' ʿUlūm al-Dīn]*. Translated by T.J. Winter. Cambridge: The Islamic Text Society, 1989, p.2.
230. Syed Ruzee: *Nahjul Balagha; Sermons, Letters and Sayings of Hazrat Ali*. Translated by Syed Mohammed Askari Jafery. India: Seerat-u-Zahra Committee, 1965, p.165.
231. Al-Ghazālī: *The Remembrance of Death and the Afterlife [Iḥyā' ʿUlūm al-Dīn]*. Translated by T.J. Winter. Cambridge: The Islamic Text Society, 1989, p.30.
232. Vincent. J. Cornell: *The Way of Abū Madyan – The Works of Abū Madyan*. Cambridge: The Islamic Text Society, 1996, p.118.
233. Imām ʿAbdullāh ibn ʿAlawī al-Ḥaddād: *Knowledge and Wisdom*. Translated by Mostafa al-Badawi. Illinois: Starlatch Press, 2001, p.30.

234. Shaykh ʿAbd al-Qādir al-Jīlānī: *The Removal of Cares [Jalā' al-Khawāṭir – A Collection of Forty Discourses.]* Translated by Muhtar Holland. Fort Lauderdale: Al-Baz Publishing Inc, 1997, p.143.
235. Al-Ghazālī: *The Remembrance of Death and the Afterlife [Iḥyā' ʿUlūm al-Dīn].* Translated by T.J. Winter. Cambridge: The Islamic Text Society, 1989, p.27.
236. Ibn Ḥazm al-Andalusī: *In Pursuit of Virtue.* London: Taha Publishers, 1990, p.138.
237. Shaykh ʿAbd al-Qādir al-Jīlānī: *The Removal of Cares [Jalā' al-Khawāṭir – A Collection of Forty Discourses].* Translated by Muhtar Holland. Fort Lauderdale: Al-Baz Publishing Inc, 1997, p.155.
238. Shaykh Muṣliḥ al-Dīn Saʿdī: *The Gulistān [Rose Garden].* Translated by Edward B Eastwick. London: The Octagon Press Ltd, 1979, p.37.
239. Al-Muqaddisī: *Revelation of the Secrets of the Birds and Flowers.* Translated by Irene Hoare & Darya Galy) London: Octagon Press, 1979, p.14.
240. At daybreak on the day of his death.
241. Al-Ghazālī: *The Remembrance of Death and the Afterlife [Iḥyā' ʿUlūm al-Dīn].* Translated by T.J. Winter. Cambridge: The Islamic Text Society, 1989, p.83.
242. On his deathbed when asked if a physician should be called.
243. Ibid: p.74.
244. Elegy on the death of the Holy Prophet, peace be upon him.
245. Prof Masud ul-Hassan: *Ṣiddīq-l-Akbar, Ḥazrat Abū Bakr.* New Delhi: Kitab Bhavan, p.23.
246. Shaykh ʿAbd al-Qādir Al-Jīlānī: *Jilā' al-Khāṭir (Purification of the Mind).* Edited by Sheikh Muhammad al-Casazani al-Husseini and translated by Prof. Shetha al-Dargazelli and Dr. Louay Fatoohi. Kuala Lumpur: A.S. Noordeen, 1999, p.135.